P9-BJL-830

International Economic Problems

Introduction to Economics Series

Kenyon A. Knopf, *Editor*

International Economic Problems

JAMES C. INGRAM
University of North Carolina

SECOND EDITION

John Wiley & Sons, Inc.
New York · London · Sydney · Toronto

HF.
1411
.I 39
1970 / 44, 809

Copyright © 1966, 1970, by John Wiley & Sons. Inc.

All rights reserved. No part of this book may be reproduced
by any means, nor transmitted, nor translated into a machine
language without the written permission of the publisher.

Library of Congress Catalogue Card Number: 76   109378

SBN 471   42790   X (Cloth) 471   42791   8 (Paper)

Printed in the United States of America

10 9 8 7 6 5 4 3 2 1

Introduction to Economics Series

Teachers of introductory economics seem to agree on the impracticality of presenting a comprehensive survey of economics to freshman or sophomores. Many of them believe there is a need for some alternative which provides a solid core of principles while permitting an instructor to introduce a select set of problems and applied ideas. This series attempts to fill that need and also to give the interested layman a set of self-contained books that he can absorb with interest and profit, without assistance.

By offering greater flexibility in the choice of topics for study, these books represent a more realistic and reasonable approach to teaching economics than most of the large, catchall textbooks. With separate volumes and different authors for each topic, the instructor is not as tied to a single track as in the omnibus introductory economics text.

Underlying the series is the pedagogical premise that students should be introduced to economics by learning how economists think about economic problems. Thus the concepts and relationships of elementary economics are presented to the student in conjunction with a few economic problems. An approach of this kind offers a good beginning to the student who intends to move on to advanced work and furnishes a clearer understanding for those whose study of economics is limited to an introductory exposure. Teachers and students alike should find the books helpful and stimulating.

Kenyon A. Knopf, Editor

7 l

DISCARDED COLLEGE LIBRARY

LEARNING RESOURCES CENTRE
ALBERTA VOCATIONAL CENTRE
CAMROSE LUTHERAN COLLEGE
CALGARY, ALBERTA

v

Preface

This preface is addressed to economists and other specialists; the book itself is addressed to students and laymen who want a compact statement of the major problems confronting the world economy. I hope that my professional colleagues will be patient with the simplifications and understanding about the omissions that must inevitably occur in a work of this kind.

Teachers of introductory courses in a variety of disciplines, notably economics, political science, and history, frequently complain that they find it difficult to obtain a reasonably comprehensive discussion of major international economic problems in convenient form. In college and university courses in the principles of economics, for example, textbooks typically include two or three chapters on international trade and finance, but these chapters are usually limited to general principles. To enable the student to see how these principles apply to contemporary problems, the instructor must assign a wide variety of additional material. All too often, limited time and library pressures cause the harried instructor to omit the extra assignments and leave the student with only the bare principles.

The purpose of this book is to supply a brief but authoritative account of three major topics in international economics: trade between advanced and underdeveloped countries, the European Economic Community, and reform of the international monetary system. As an essential preliminary to the discussion of these topics, a brief statement of the principles of international trade and monetary organization is provided.

I am grateful to all the students, instructors, and other readers who have given me their suggestions and comments about the first edition of this book. In this second edition, I have taken account of these suggestions, as far as possible. I have also brought the statistics up to date, and I have revised the discussions of policy issues to incorporate recent developments.

James C. Ingram

Contents

1

Introduction

In a single generation the United States has been catapulted into a position of leadership in the free world. Along with this leadership, the United States has fallen heir to awesome international responsibilities, both political and economic. Americans are now presented with a daily diet of headlines concerned with international economic issues, and even our domestic issues have important effects on the outside world.

Modern developments in transportation and communication have greatly increased the degree of economic interdependence among nations. Economic changes in one part of the world are rapidly transmitted to other areas. Thus, a change in the United States wheat program can have profound effects on farmers in Australia and Argentina or upon consumers in Rome or Tokyo. Similarly, technological innovations in German or Japanese firms can influence prices in American markets and thus affect firms and workers in our towns and cities. Many economic policies which we may think of as purely domestic in nature actually have substantial impacts upon the outside world.

The size and strength of the United States economy are so great that the nation is intimately involved in economic issues throughout the world. The United States alone accounts for over 40% of total industrial production in the free world. Even though our exports constitute only 4% of our gross national product, they constitute about 18% of total world exports. The enormous market of the United States absorbs a large part of the commodities

1

that other countries want to sell. For example, American consumers buy over one half of world coffee exports, and American
industry purchases about one half of world exports of tin, rubber,
and many other products. The United States has also made large
investments in foreign countries; it is the major source of loans
and grants to underdeveloped countries; and it plays an important role in world banking and finance. When the dollar is
under pressure, as it has been in recent years, the stability of
the entire world monetary system is placed in jeopardy.

Whether we like it or not, every action of the United States
is of interest and concern to all other nations, and the United
States is affected by actions taken by other nations. The informed
citizen in such an interdependent world needs to have an understanding of the nature of economic problems confronting the
world economy and, as a basis for that understanding, he needs
a framework of analysis within which the problems may be
studied.

In the following chapters we shall set forth some basic principles of international economics and use them to analyze and
explain several important issues of international economic policy.
"International economics" is not a separate and distinct field
of study; it is just plain economics applied to the trade and
financial relationships among nations. The concepts and techniques studied in the principles of economics clearly have their
application to international economic problems.

The plan of this book is as follows. Chapters 2 and 4 contain
an explanation of some basic principles of international trade
and monetary organization. For many readers, these chapters,
especially Chapter 2, will be the most difficult part of the book.
The reader should persevere, however, because mastery of these
principles will give him a surer grasp of the problems to follow.
Chapters 5 to 7 are devoted to three of the most important issues
or problems in the world economy at the present time. These
issues are: (1) trade relations between advanced and underdeveloped countries, an aspect of the "revolution of rising expectations" in the poor countries of the world, (2) the emergence
of the European Common Market and its probable effects upon
the outside world, both rich and poor, and (3) the continuing
crisis in the world monetary system, with gold and the dollar

deficits the immediate crux of the matter. A fourth issue, the perennial tariff question, is discussed more briefly in Chapter 3.

These issues are highly topical. They are intimately bound up with political and social aspects, but they can scarcely be understood without a firm grasp of the underlying economic principles. Although economic analysis does not yield clear and definite conclusions on the major policy questions involved in these issues, it provides useful insights and enables the nature of the problems to be understood.

These issues are large and complex, and many books have been written about each of them. The purpose of this book is not to give an exhaustive account of any of them, but to provide an introductory account that will encourage the reader to pursue the matter in greater depth.

2

Why Nations Trade

Nations trade with each other because they benefit from it. Other motives may be involved, of course, but the basic economic motivation for international trade is that of *gain*. The gain from international trade, like the gain from all trade, exists because specialization increases productivity. We are familiar with the fruits of specialization and the division of labor in trade between regions of a single country, or between persons in a town, but we may not perceive that the same benefits exist in international trade. The political boundaries that divide geographic areas into nations do not change the fundamental nature of trade and the benefits it confers on the trading partners. Our task in this chapter is to establish and illustrate this basic truth.

I. TRADE AND EXCHANGE BETWEEN PERSONS

In the modern world, all of us depend upon other people to produce a large part of the goods and services we consume. A man may think of himself as independent and self-reliant, but he probably satisfies most of his material needs by selling his services or his own specialized output in the market, buying in exchange a variety of goods and services for his own use. We may be intrigued by Thoreau and Robinson Crusoe, but few of us are prepared to accept the standard of living that genuine self-sufficiency implies.

As a mental experiment, imagine that a single family (the

Smiths) undertakes to become completely self-sufficient. Smith vows to have "no truck" with the rest of the economy, to sell no part of his produce and to buy nothing whatsoever—no fertilizer, gasoline, repair parts, tools, or anything. Suppose that Smith finds 160 acres of fertile, well-watered land to homestead; allow him the enormous advantage of an initial stock of clothing, tools, equipment, household goods, and other supplies. A little reflection will probably convince us that no matter how skillful and industrious Smith and his family may be, they will be unable to produce, through their own efforts, the necessities of life (bread, meat, sugar, fruit, clothing, shoes, and light), not to mention such frills as medicine, television, lipstick, books, or carbonated beverages. Their initial stock of supplies will inexorably shrink, even though conserved and patched, and their standard of living will sink to a low level. At best, they will be able to eke out a hard, mean existence, and even that will be at the mercy of weather and disease. Yet Smith might, with exactly the same skill, energy, and resources, achieve a comfortable standard of living if he specialized in the production of a small number of products, selling these and buying other products for his family's use.

Suppose, for example, that wheat is one of Smith's principal crops. If he specializes in wheat, he can produce 8000 bushels per year. To supply the shoes that his family needs, Smith can sell 75 bushels of wheat for $2 per bushel and buy 10 pairs of shoes at an average price of $15 per pair (75 bushels @ $2 = $150 = 10 pairs of shoes @ $15). If he tries to make the shoes himself, he must spend less time on his wheat crop, and it will fall by (for example) 600 bushels. The real cost of making shoes by hand is measured by the fall in wheat output. In this case, what economists call the "opportunity cost" of 10 pairs of shoes is 600 bushels of wheat. Thus we can compare the cost of obtaining shoes in two different ways:

Cost of 10 Pairs of Shoes

Through trade	75 bushels
Through direct production (opportunity cost)	600 bushels

If Smith devotes his efforts to wheat production, he can buy 10 pairs of shoes and still have 525 bushels of wheat (600 − 75) to use for other purchases. Alternatively, in the time that it takes him to make 10 pairs of shoes by hand, he could produce 600 bushels of wheat that he could exchange for 80 pairs of shoes.

This simple principle of opportunity-cost comparison applies to a great variety of choices at many levels: individuals, business firms, and nations. Should an expert engineer do his own drafting or hire a draftsman? Should a student spend 10 hours typing his own term paper or work 2 hours to earn the money to hire a typist? Should a shoe factory generate its own electricity or use the funds to expand its output of shoes? Should Scotland produce wine, even though "by means of glasses, hotbeds, and hotwalls, very good grapes can be raised in Scotland, and very good wine too can be made of them at about thirty times the expense for which at least equally good can be brought from foreign countries."?[1]

Adam Smith dramatized the benefits of trade and the division of labor, for both individuals and nations, in the following passage.[2]

It is the maxim of every prudent master of a family, never to attempt to make at home what it will cost him more to make than to buy. The taylor does not attempt to make his own shoes, but buys them of the shoemaker. The shoemaker does not attempt to make his own clothes but employs a taylor. The farmer attempts to make neither the one nor the other, but employs those different artificers. All of them find it for their interest to employ their whole industry in a way in which they have some advantage over their neighbours, and to purchase with a part of its produce, or what is the same thing, with the price of a part of it, whatever else they have occasion for.

II. TRADE BETWEEN NATIONS

Nations, like individuals, should specialize in the production of the goods that they can make with relatively greatest efficiency. Through such specialization and trade, they can each obtain a

---

[1] Adam Smith, *The Wealth of Nations* (New York: The Modern Library, 1937), p. 425.
[2] Smith, op. cit., p. 424.

larger amount of consumable goods than they would have without trade.

Sometimes a nation cannot possibly produce a given product because it does not possess the necessary natural resources or because of climate. For example, the United States possesses no known deposits of tin ore, and we must import the tin that we need from other countries. Our soil and climate are not suitable for growing tea; thus, to keep our tea-drinkers happy, we import $57 million (1966) worth of tea from India, Ceylon, and other tea producers. Much international trade is based on such unequal geographic distribution of minerals, soil types, and rainfall. The benefit of this trade is obvious to all, and its desirability is rarely questioned.

The more difficult cases concern those situations in which two countries can both produce the same commodities. Our problem is to show that the advantages of specialization and exchange are still present. (The alert reader may object, at this point, that the above distinction is not sharply drawn. Tea *could* be produced in the United States if we were willing to devote enough energy and resources to its cultivation. We could even "mine" tin from scrap heaps and junkyards, and thereby supply new tin for industrial use. The reader is correct; the difference is usually one of degree, although in popular usage we often speak as if it were absolute.)

Consider a simple example to illustrate the basic principle. Suppose that Germany is producing only two commodities: wheat and steel. German resources are fully employed, and the conditions of production are such that if wheat output increases 5 tons, steel output drops 5 tons. That is, we assume that a given package of resources can produce 5 tons of wheat or 5 tons of steel.[3] The opportunity cost of 1 ton of steel is 1 ton of wheat, and vice

[3] The practical reader may be appalled at the suggestion that resources released from wheat production could be transferred to steel production. The example is illustrative, not fully realistic, but we should note that more substitutability in resource use exists than may appear at first sight. If Germany curtailed wheat production, resources used to make agricultural machinery, fertilizer, farm buildings, and the like, would be released for use in expanding the steel industry. Labor released from agriculture would move into towns and cities. Even if the farm laborers did not go directly into steel, they would release other workers, for instance, in service industries, for employment in steel.

versa. To start with, assume that Germany has no foreign trade.

Now if the opportunity arises to trade with the rest of the world
(ROW) at an exchange ratio different from her domestic ratio
($1S = 1W$), Germany can benefit from trade. For example, suppose that the exchange ratio between steel and wheat in ROW is
$1S = 2W$, and suppose that Germany is so small in relation to
ROW that German sales of steel have no effect on world prices.
Comparing Germany's domestic ratio to the world exchange ratio,
we can see that Germany has a *comparative* advantage in steel.
That is, its cost of steel (measured in terms of wheat given up) is
less than in the outside world. Note that we do not need to know
whether German labor is efficient or inefficient compared to labor
in other countries. Foreign producers may use 10 times as much
labor (or one-tenth as much) as German producers, but all that
matters to Germany is that it can obtain more wheat through trade
than through direct production at home. It will pay Germany to
shift resources out of wheat and into steel, using the increased
steel output to buy wheat in ROW (we shall ignore transport
costs for the time being). For every ton of wheat lost through
curtailed production, Germany can obtain 2 tons through trade.
Germany's gain from trade lies in its ability to obtain wheat at less
cost in resources than it would cost at home. Some gain will exist
as long as the exchange ratio in ROW *differs* from Germany's
domestic ratio. That is, with a domestic ratio of $1S = 1W$,
Germany will benefit as long as it can get anything more than
1 ton of wheat for 1 ton of steel.[4] Only if the external exchange
ratio is exactly equal to Germany's ratio ($1S = 1W$) will there
be no opportunity for gainful trade.

This example can be conveniently illustrated through use of
the "production possibility curve." Suppose that if *all* Germany's
resources were put into wheat-growing, its total output would be
100 million tons. Germany would then produce no steel. If resources capable of producing 10 million tons of steel were taken
out of wheat growing, the output of wheat would drop by 10
million tons. (This follows from our assumption that a given
package of resources can produce 5 tons of wheat or 5 tons of

---

[4] If 1 ton of steel buys *less* than 1 ton of wheat in ROW, Germany will
benefit by trading wheat for steel.

Table 2-1. Alternative Combinations of Wheat and Steel that Germany Can Produce.

(Millions of Tons)

Wheat:	100	90	80	70	60	50	40	30	20	10	0
Steel:	0	10	20	30	40	50	60	70	80	90	100

steel in Germany.) If all German resources were shifted to steel production, total output would be 100 million tons of steel and *no* wheat. We can now draw up a list (Table 2-1) of a number of alternative combinations of wheat and steel that Germany could produce. In this example we assume that opportunity costs remain constant; that is, every increase of 10 million tons of steel requires a reduction of 10 million tons of wheat, and vice versa. These facts can also be shown in a diagram (Figure 2-1). The figure contains the same information as Table 2-1. The straight line *AB* represents the "production possibility curve" for the German economy. Points along the line *AB* represent combinations of wheat and steel that Germany can produce at full employment. At *A*, it produces 100 wheat and no steel; at *B*, 100 steel and no wheat; at *P*, 60 wheat and 40 steel. That *AB* is a straight line indicates that opportunity cost remains constant (1S = 1W) as Germany shifts resources from one industry to the other. The *slope* of *AB* is equal to the domestic ratio of exchange. The line *AB*, therefore, represents the highest attainable outputs the German economy can produce at full employment. All points to the right of *AB* represent combinations of wheat and steel that are beyond the reach of German capacity. (What can you say about a point to the left of *AB*, such as *Q*?) In a market economy, consumers will decide at what point along *AB* the economy will actually operate. If they want more wheat and less steel, they will bid up the price of wheat, and businessmen will shift resources from steel to wheat. We shall assume that, when Germany has no trade with the rest of the world, German consumers prefer the combination at point *P*. At *P*, German production (60W and 40S) equals German consumption.

Production (Net National Product) = *Consumption*

Wheat: 60 million tons	Wheat: 60 million tons
Steel: 40 million tons	Steel: 40 million tons

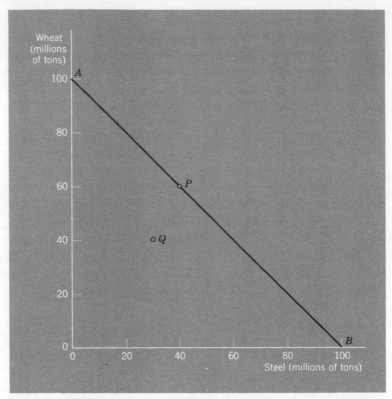

Figure 2-1. German production possibilities. The line *AB* shows how many tons of wheat that Germany can produce at each level of steel production. If Germany produces 40 steel, it can also produce 60 wheat; this combination is indicated by the point *P*. The slope of *AB* represents the rate at which steel can be transformed into wheat by a shift in resources from steel production to wheat production.

We can now show what happens when the opportunity arises to trade with ROW and exchange 1 ton of steel for 2 tons of wheat. In Figure 2-2 we add the trading-possibility line, *CB*, drawn with a slope equal to the exchange ratio in ROW (1S = 2W). The opening up of trade enlarges the range of choice available to German consumers. It makes possible the choice of some combinations of wheat and steel that formerly lay beyond their reach. All those combinations lying between *AB* and *CB* (in the elongated triangle *ACB*) are now available to German consumers.

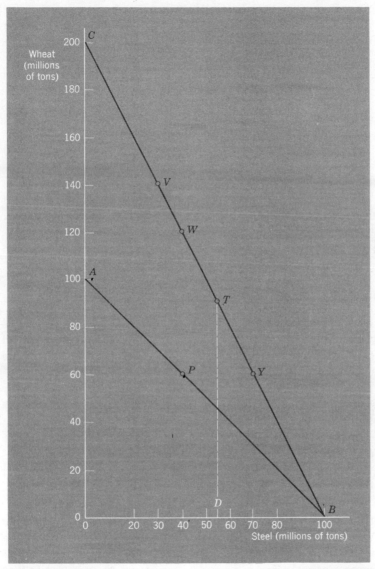

Figure 2-2. Trade between Germany and the rest of the world. Before trade, Germany produced 40 steel and 60 wheat, consuming all that it produced. Given the opportunity to trade one steel for two wheat (along the line *BC*), Germany produces *OB* (100) of steel, exporting *DB* (45) of it to buy *DT* (90) of wheat from ROW. Germany then consumes *OD* (55) of steel and *DT* (90) of wheat.

If Germany specializes in steel (produces at B), it can trade steel for wheat and move along the "trade possibility" line CB to whatever point its consumers prefer. For example, if their preference is for the point T, Germany can trade 45S for 90W and therefore obtain more of both commodities than it had before trade. To reach point T, Germany exports DB of steel (45) in exchange for DT of wheat (90). We can summarize the German position as follows:

Production (NNP)	−	*Exports*	+	*Imports*	=	*Consumption*
Wheat 0	−	0	+	90	=	90W
Steel 100	−	45	+	0	=	55S

Germany's gain from trade can easily be seen by comparing the amount of goods retained for domestic use before and after trade:

	Before Trade	*After Trade*
Wheat:	60 million tons	90 million tons
Steel	40 million tons	55 million tons

Since population and resources employed remain the same, Germany clearly can increase economic welfare in the sense of providing everyone with more material goods than he had before trade began.

The alert student may now ask how we can claim that Germany has a clear gain if it chooses a point such as V on the trading-possibility line CB, where Germany has more of one good but less of the other than before trade. At V, Germany retains 140W and 30S for its own use—more wheat but less steel than before trade. Can we be sure that Germany has gained? A partial answer is that if Germany chooses the point V it must prefer more wheat and less steel. After all, Germany has the opportunity to choose *any* point on CB: it could choose T and have more of both commodities; it could choose W and have the same amount of steel as at P but more wheat. At the price $1S = 2W$ Germany can obtain as much or more steel than it had before trade, and the fact that it chooses less steel indicates that consumers prefer less now that they can swap steel for wheat on favorable terms. Another part of the answer is that at the trading ratio $1S = 2W$ Germany could, if it wished, attain its pretrade

level of consumption (60W and 40S) and still have real output
left over. That is, Germany could produce 100 steel, trade 30S
for 60W, and thus retain for domestic use 60W and 70S. At this
position (point Y in Figure 2-2) it can consume at the pretrade
level and still have 30S left over. This additional amount of steel
can be consumed at home, traded for wheat, or even traded for
leisure in the sense that Germany could achieve the pretrade level
(P) by using fewer resources with trade, perhaps taking the gain
from trade in shorter work weeks.

Thus far, we have examined the position of one country, and
we have assumed that that country has the opportunity to trade at
a fixed world exchange ratio between steel and wheat. We assumed that Germany's offer of steel on the world market did not
affect the world terms-of-trade ratio. We shall now consider a
case in which we have two countries of approximately equal size.
This will enable us to show how the terms of trade may be
changed when trade begins. We can also show that *both* parties
can gain from international trade.

Our two countries are Germany and France. The German production-possibility curve remains the same as in Figure 2-1. We
assume that France can produce 240 million tons of wheat or
80 million tons of steel if it specializes fully in one or the other.
The French production possibility curve is shown in Figure 2-3
as the line *HJ*. It is a straight line, indicating constant opportunity
cost, and the domestic exchange ratio in France is 1S = 3W. We
assume that in the absence of trade French consumers prefer the
point K, where 120W and 40S are produced and consumed.

Before trade, the domestic terms of trade differ in our two
countries: in Germany, 1S = 1W; in France, 1S = 3W. We saw
above that Germany benefits when it can exchange 1S for anything more than 1W; now we can also see that France will benefit
if it can obtain 1S for anything *less* than 3W, which is the domestic cost.

When trade begins between our two countries, the terms of
trade may lie anywhere between the two domestic ratios, anywhere between 1S = 1W and 1S = 3W. For example, suppose
the trading terms of trade were 1S = 2W. We have already seen
that Germany will specialize in steel, and let us suppose that
German consumers prefer the point T on their trading-possibility

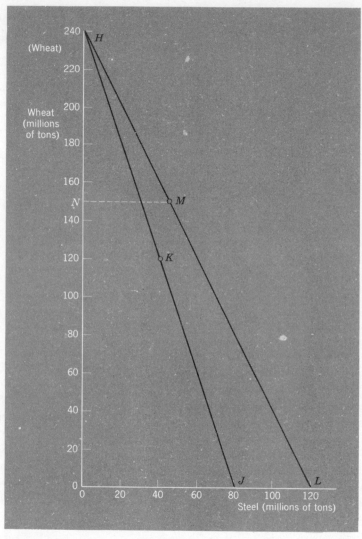

Figure 2-3. French production possibilities and a trading opportunity. The line *HJ* shows how many tons of wheat France can produce at each level of steel production. Before trade, France produced 40 steel and 120 wheat (the point *K*). The French domestic exchange ratio is 1 steel for 3 wheat. Given the opportunity to trade at the ratio $1S = 2W$ (along the line *HL*), France produces *OH* (240) of wheat, exporting *HN* (90) of it to buy *NM* (45) of steel from Germany.

line *CB* (see Figure 2-2), at which point Germany desires to export 45S and import 90W.

Now the question is: How much wheat will France wish to export at the terms of trade 1S = 2W? On Figure 2-3 we draw the line *HL* to represent France's trading-possibility curve. It originates at *H* because France will specialize in wheat production. We see that, by trading wheat for steel, France can move along *HL* and obtain combinations of output that lie beyond its reach *through* domestic production. If French consumers prefer the point *M*, they will export 90W in exchange for 45S. The French production-consumption position will then appear as follows:

Production (NNP)	−	Exports	+	Imports	=	Consumption
Wheat: 240	−	90	+	0	=	150
Steel: 0	−	0	+	45	=	45

Comparison of the amounts of goods retained for domestic use before and after trade shows that France has gained from trade:

	Before Trade	After Trade
Wheat:	120 million tons	150 million tons
Steel:	40 million tons	45 million tons

We saw, above, that Germany also gains from trade at the terms-of-trade ratio 1S = 2W, and thus it comes as no surprise to find that world output of both commodities increases as a result of trade. Table 2-2 contains a summary of the world position before and after trade. Before trade, world outputs of wheat and steel were 180W and 80S; post-trade outputs are 240W and 100S. By what magic has world output of both these commodities increased without the use of any additional resources? The answer is that specialization—the use of each nation's resources to produce the commodity in which it possesses a comparative advantage—has made possible a larger total output than can be achieved under self-sufficiency.

In our example, at the exchange ratio 1S = 2W, France wanted to export exactly the amount of wheat that Germany wanted to import. What happens if the desired levels of wheat exports and imports do not match so conveniently? The answer is that the exchange ratio must *change*. For example, if France wanted to

Table 2-2. The Gain from Trade—Summary Showing Production and Consumption in Each Country before and after Trade

	Wheat Production − Exports + Imports = Consumption					Steel Production − Exports + Imports = Consumption				
Situation before Trade										
France	120				120	40				40
Germany	60				60	40				40
Total world	180				180	80				80
Situation after Trade										
France	240	− 90	+ 0	=	150	0	− 0	+ 45		45
Germany	0	− 0	+ 90	=	90	100	− 45	+ 0		55
Total world	240				240	100				100
Gain from Trade										
France					+ 30					+ 5
Germany					+ 30					+ 15
Total world					+ 60					+ 20

export only 50 wheat at the ratio $1S = 2W$, while Germany wanted to buy 90 wheat at that ratio, the excess demand for wheat would cause its price (value in terms of steel) to rise. That is, more steel would be offered for wheat, and the exchange ratio would move toward $1.1S = 2W$, and so on. As wheat becomes dearer to German buyers, their demand for wheat imports will fall, while French sellers will be induced by the higher price to offer somewhat more wheat. At some point, the French offer of wheat will exactly match the German demand for wheat, and that will be an equilibrium exchange ratio. (If supply and demand exactly match for wheat, what about steel?) Graphically, we show the shifting exchange ratio by rotating the line HL, holding the point H constant, as portrayed in Figure 2-4. As the trading terms of trade move from HL to HL' and HL'', a given amount of wheat exchanges for larger and larger amounts of steel.

A. *Increasing Costs*

We can now drop the assumption that constant opportunity costs exist in our two countries. As resources are shifted from wheat to steel production, we assume that the cost of an additional ton of steel will rise. More wheat output will have to be given up to secure additional tons of steel. Instead of being a straight line, as in Figure 2-2, the German production-possibility frontier will be a curve (convex from above), as in Figure 2-5. The curvature of WPS in Figure 2-5 reflects the increasing cost of producing additional tons of steel as production shifts from P toward S.

Before trade, suppose Germany chooses to produce at the point P, where its internal exchange ratio is equal to the slope of AB, $1S = 1W$. If the opportunity to trade at the ratio $1S = 2W$ again arises, German production will shift from P to R, but Germany will not become *fully* specialized in steel production. At R the German domestic cost ratio (the slope of $WPRS$ at R) is equal to the slope of DE, the trading terms of trade $1S = 2W$, and German producers no longer have any incentive to shift resources from wheat to steel. If German consumers want to consume at the point T, Germany will export TV of steel and import RV of wheat. If the trading partner, France, wants to export wheat and import steel in corresponding quantities, trade will be in equilibrium at the exchange ratio $1S = 2W$. If not, the ex-

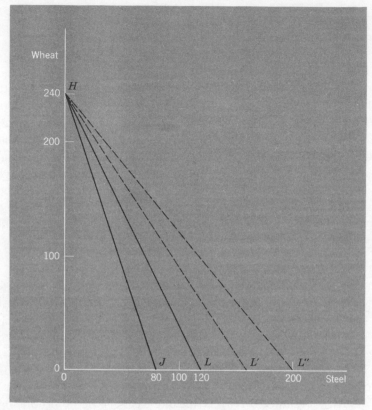

Figure 2-4. Shifts in the terms of trade. As the line *HL* shifts to *HL′ and HL″*, a given amount of wheat exchanges for larger amounts of steel. The terms of trade improve for wheat producers.

change ratio must change, as before, until German exports of steel match French imports of steel (and German wheat imports match French wheat exports).

Trade brings additional combinations of the two commodities within the reach of a country's consumers. In Figure 2-5, for example, Germany can produce by its own efforts any combination of steel and wheat lying on (or below) the production-possibility curve *WPS*. If it can trade at the exchange ratio $1S = 2W$, however, Germany can obtain any combination of steel and wheat lying on the line *DE*. The opportunity to trade thus expands the range of choice available to German consumers.

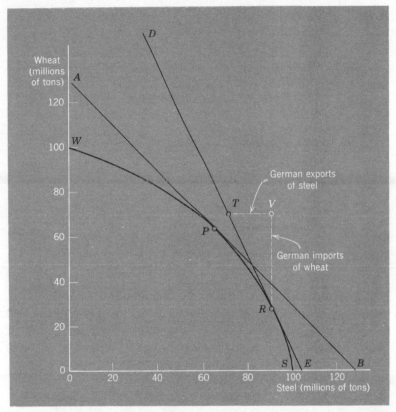

Figure 2-5. German trade under conditions of increasing costs. As Germany expands its steel production, the cost of steel rises in terms of foreign wheat. If Germany can trade at the trading ratio $1S = 2W$ (slope of DE), German production will shift to R, and Germany will export TV of steel to buy RV of wheat.

B. *The Role of Money Prices*

In the modern world, traders actually place their orders and strike bargains on the basis of money prices, not the barter ratios that we have examined thus far. Traders buy a foreign good when its price is lower than at home. (We are still ignoring transport costs, but traders must allow for them and for all other costs—tariff, insurance, commissions, legal costs, etc.—in comparing domestic and foreign prices.) A German wheat importer pays no attention to the barter ratio between steel and wheat, and he may be oblivious to opportunity cost as we have used it above. Nevertheless, the basic principles on which trade is based, principles laid bare in our simple barter examples, will still apply when we bring in money prices.

A barter exchange ratio, such as we have used in our example of trade between France and Germany, implies a ratio of *money* prices. For example, if one apple exchanges for two oranges, the price of an apple is twice the price of an orange (if an apple costs 10¢ and an orange costs 5¢, then one apple = two oranges). Therefore, if barter exchange ratios differ in two countries, *relative* money prices will also differ.

W can use the French-German constant cost example to illustrate this point. Before trade, the domestic (barter) exchange ratios were:

France: 1 ton of steel = 3 tons of wheat
Germany: 1 ton of steel = 1 ton of wheat

The money price in France of 1 ton of steel is therefore equal to the money price of 3 tons of wheat. That is, 1 ton of steel costs 3 times as much as 1 ton of wheat. In Germany, the money price of 1 ton of steel is equal to the money price of 1 ton of wheat. We assume the following actual money prices in the two countries.

		France	*Germany*
Steel	(per ton)	Francs 300	Marks 400
Wheat	(per ton)	Francs 100	Marks 400
Ratio	$\left[\dfrac{\text{price of steel}}{\text{price of wheat}} \right]$	3/1	1/1

Note that the ratio of prices is different in the two countries (3/1 in France, 1/1 in Germany). This is what we mean by *relative* prices being different. Such relative price differences mirror the differences in opportunity cost ratios in our barter example, and they tell us that an opportunity for gainful trade exists.

These are the money prices prevailing before trade begins. When trade opens up, how can traders compare prices? Will German buyers wish to buy French steel at 300 francs per ton? Or will French buyers find German steel a bargain at 400 marks a ton? Since the currencies used are different, we must know the exchange rate between francs and marks before meaningful price comparisons can be made. The exchange rate is a price, a rate at which we can convert one currency into another. If the exchange rate is franc 1.00 = mark 2.00, French buyers can compare German prices with their own: German steel will cost them fr. 200 per ton (fr. 200 = mk. 400) compared to fr. 300 at home; German wheat will cost fr. 200 per ton compared to fr. 100 at home. French traders will therefore import steel and export wheat. At the same time, German traders will find French wheat cheaper (fr. 100 @ mk. 2 = mk. 200) than domestic wheat. Thus, a *two-way* trade, profitable to both sides, will spring up: German steel will exchange for French wheat, although each trader is simply pursuing his own individual interest in buying at the cheapest possible price.

The next question is: Will French imports of steel be equal in *money value* to German imports of wheat? If so, we will have balanced trade; if not, the imbalance in trade will cause the exchange rate to shift. In our barter example, above, we had France import 45 million tons of steel and export 90 million tons of wheat. The money value of its trade, at the prices we have used above, would therefore be:

Wheat exports, 90 million tons @ fr. 100 = fr. 9000 million
Steel imports, 45 million tons @ fr. 200 = fr. 9000 million

Thus we have a position of balanced trade in money value, just as we did in barter terms.

If French exports did not equal imports in money value, the exchange rate would change.[5] For example, if German traders wanted to buy 100 million tons of French wheat when the exchange rate was fr. 1 = mk. 2, they would try to buy fr. 10,000 million in the foreign-exchange market, but French traders would be offering only fr. 9000 million for German steel. The excess demand for francs would drive up their price—that is, 1 franc would exchange for somewhat more than 2 marks, for example, fr. 1 = mk. 2.5. Keeping money prices the same in the two

[5] In our analysis thus far, we have assumed that commodity trade is the only form of economic transaction occurring between nations. Later we shall allow for trade in services, and for gifts, capital movements, and other transactions.

The foreign-exchange market would be in equilibrium at fr. 1 = mk. 2, and at this exchange rate prices are the same at home and abroad. Hence, no basis for trade would exist.

C. *Causes of Relative Price Differences*

We have shown that trade rests upon differences in relative prices. But *why* do relative prices differ between countries? The principal explanation lies in the uneven distribution of world resources among nations, coupled with the fact that commodities require different proportions of the factors of production. The uneven distribution of productive resources is partly a matter of climate and geography, and partly a result of each nation's historical development which has left it with a certain stock of capital and a population trained and educated in numerous skills and techniques. When a nation possesses an abundance of the factors of production required to produce a commodity, its price for that commodity will be low relative to its price for another commodity requiring much of productive factors that are scarce—low, that is, in comparison to the same ratio in another country.

In our example, suppose steel requires relatively much capital and little land, while wheat requires much land and little capital. In France, we assume that wheat land is plentiful and capital scarce, while in Germany wheat land is scarce and capital abundant. In the absence of trade, France must produce her own steel, which requires much of her scarce capital. The resulting heavy demand for scarce French capital bids up the price of capital services, and maker steel an expensive commodity, especially in comparison to wheat, which uses much of the abundant (and, therefore, cheap!) French land. In Germany, before trade, the opposite situation prevails, and we can thus see why the *ratio* of French prices (price of steel/price of wheat) will likely be greater than the ratio of German prices. Relative prices differ because prices before trade reflect the unequal factor endowments of two countries.

Factor endowments in each country determine the position and *shape* of the production-possibility curve in each country. In France, where land is abundant and capital scarce, the production-possibility curve is elongated on the wheat axis, as in Figure 2-6, indicating the suitability of French resources for producing

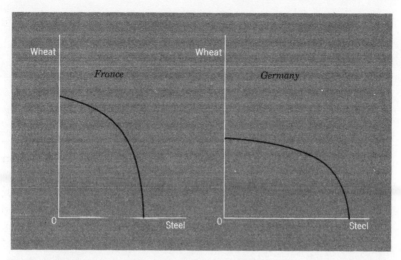

Figure 2-6. Different factor endowments in France and Germany affect the shape of the production-possibility curves. The abundance of land in France causes France's production-possibility curve to be biased toward wheat production, compared to Germany, where abundant capital biases the production-possibility curve toward steel production.

land-intensive wheat. Germany's production-possibility curve is biased more toward steel production, reflecting her greater abundance of capital.

Many familiar examples of differences in factor endowment pertain to natural resources and such environmental characteristics as temperature, rainfall, and humidity. Rich deposits of minerals—copper in Chile, petroleum in the Middle East, tin in Malaya—give these areas an obvious "relative abundance" of a productive factor. Similarly, tropical countries have a relative abundance (compared to temperate-zone countries) of environmental factors (climate and rainfall) required for the production of bananas, mangoes, coffee, and other tropical foodstuffs. As Samuelson has remarked, only partly in jest, "The tropics grow tropical fruits because of the relative abundance there of tropical conditions."[6] Compared with Belgium, Australia has abundant land and scarce labor. Australia has 190 acres of land per capita,

[6] P. A. Samuelson, "International Trade and the Equalization of Factor Prices," *Economic Journal,* June 1948, p. 182.

Belgium has less than 1 acre. Australian exports, therefore, include many land-intensive products such as wheat, meat, and wool, while Belgian exports include products requiring much skilled labor and capital, such as machinery and textiles.

In the United States, capital per worker is about $15000; in India it is about $1000. Thus, in trade between the United States and India, we expect to find the United States exporting relatively capital intensive products (for example, machinery) and importing labor-intensive products (for example, needlework, handloomed rugs, and textiles).

Such broad aggregative comparisons are helpful and suggestive, but to explain much international trade we must use a much finer and more detailed classification of the factors of production. Instead of a single broad category "labor," we actually have hundreds of specific types of labor, each involving a special skill, talent, or level of education. At any given time, nations have different relative supplies of such specific types of labor, and these different supplies form the basis of much international specialization and exchange. Switzerland has a relative abundance of watchmakers; Sweden a relative abundance of glass-blowers; France a relative abundance of vintners. Similarly, the broad categories "land," "capital," and "entrepreneurship" break down into a large number of specific subfactors. Land is a catch-all term for a great variety of soil types, minerals and other natural resources, moisture, temperature, and other climatic factors, while capital means the specific form of equipment and structures used in the production of a commodity. Every type of machine is a separate subfactor within the broad category "capital." The actual structure of world trade is therefore the outcome of millions of factor-proportion comparisons in thousands of commodities. The awesome complexity of this structure makes us turn to highly simplified two-country, two-commodity examples in search of a principle that will illuminate the problem.

We should note that factor endowments are not fixed and immutable. Labor can be trained; new forms of capital can be made or bought; even land can be changed in its role as a factor of production through irrigation, drainage, or enrichment. In our examples we took the stock of factors as given, and so it is at any point in time, but it is capable of change. This point is especially pertinent in considering the relationship between trade and development.

Our explanation of different relative prices has two parts: (1) unequal relative endowments of productive factors, just discussed, and (2) the technological condition that commodities require different factor-proportions in their production. What do we mean by this second condition? Can you think of any products that absolutely require a high proportion of capital? Even in terms of the broad categories "labor" and "capital," some commodities can be labeled as more capital-intensive than others. High-octane gasoline, synthetic fibers (such as nylon, orlon), and stainless-steel sheets are products that can be produced only with immense amounts of capital and relatively little labor, compared to labor-intensive products such as lace, textiles, or hand-blown glass. In the capital-intensive products, capital and labor can be substituted for each other, but the range of such substitution is limited. Even if labor were free, it could not replace the heavy concentration of capital required to produce steel. For any given prices of capital and labor, we therefore expect steel production to use a higher ratio of capital to labor than cotton textiles. (In the late 1950s, the Chinese government promoted the use of "backyard steel furnaces" in an attempt to produce steel with much labor and little capital, and thus utilize China's abundant labor supply. The experiment failed, apparently because the technology of steel-making required a higher ratio of capital to labor than the Chinese villagers could muster. The steel produced was poor and uneven in quality and turned out to be quite expensive.)

Given the presently known levels of technique, products require different proportions of factors in their production. Since, under competition, factor prices will be the same in all lines of production, we have a clear basis for ranking products in order of factor intensity. That is, we can say that one product is capital intensive relative to another in the sense that, when both products are produced in a nation, the first will always be produced with a higher ratio of capital to labor than the second.

When we consider specific subfactors within the broad categories, it is readily apparent that commodities require different factor proportions. Indeed, it is painfully obvious that watches require a higher proportion of watchmaker labor than bricks do, or that copper ingots require a higher proportion of copper-bearing ore than wheat. Nations thus have opportunities to specialize in products in which they have a comparative advantage—that is, products requiring relatively much of those specific factors of which they have an abundant supply.

Note that technological progress may change the basis for comparative advantage in a commodity by changing the factor-mix required for its production. For example, rubber formerly required a certain combination of soil, temperature, rainfall, and large quantities of unskilled labor, but now synthetic rubber can also be produced by a highly capital-intensive process, using small amounts of highly skilled labor. Climate is almost irrelevant. National comparative advantages are, therefore, not permanent. They may change as a nation's factor supplies change, for example, through population growth, capital formation, education and training, and as technology changes. When a shift occurs in comparative advantage, a nation may begin to export a product that it formerly imported, or vice versa.

D. *The Effects of Trade*

First, trade tends to equalize relative prices in the trading countries. (We are still ignoring transport costs.) When trade begins, traders buy more of the commodity that is relatively cheap in each country, thus increasing its price. When the flow of trade has grown large enough to eliminate relative price differences, no further increases in exports and imports will occur. In our Franco-German example, the barter terms of trade became $1S = 2W$ in both countries. Money prices are also equalized, given the exchange rate between the two currencies. When trade was balanced at the exchange rate fr. $1 =$ mk. 2, we saw that relative money prices in France

$$\left(\begin{array}{ll} \text{Steel:} & \text{fr. } 200 \\ \text{Wheat:} & \text{fr. } 100 \end{array} \right)$$

were equal to those in Germany

$$\left(\begin{array}{ll} \text{Steel:} & \text{mk. } 400 \\ \text{Wheat:} & \text{mk. } 200 \end{array} \right).$$

Differences in relative prices cause trade to take place; the flow of trade eliminates those differences and equalizes relative prices.

A second effect of trade is to reallocate resources in the two countries. Output expands in comparative advantage industries, pulling resources away from industries in which the country has a comparative disadvantage. Graphically, we see this effect as a movement along the production-possibility curve—for example, the movement in Figure 2-5 from *P* to *R*. Under conditions of increasing costs, as resources shift into the comparative advantage industry, marginal cost increases in that industry and falls in the industry whose output is contracting. The shift in resources will stop when the domestic ratio of marginal cost becomes equal to the world exchange ratio, as at R in Figure 2-5. Complete specialization will not occur in such cases. Only in the constant-cost case, where marginal costs do not change as resources move from one industry to another, will specialization go all the way.

A third effect of trade is its impact on *factor* prices. When trade begins, output expands in the industry that uses a lot of the abundant factor. Hence, demand for the abundant factor increases, and so does its price. At the same time, the scarce factor is being released from the comparative disadvantage industry, and its price must fall to encourage producers to employ it. In our example, German demand for cheap French wheat brings an increased demand for abundant wheat land in France, and thus causes its price to rise. As the French steel industry reduces output, it releases capital that must seek employment in wheat-growing, where it is less in demand. Abundant factors rise in price, and scarce factors fall in price, in each country. By redirecting world demand toward the abundant factor in each country, trade tends to equalize relative factor prices in the two countries.[7]

All of these effects of trade are a consequence of the redirection of demand that trade brings. A country's abundant factor is no longer dependent upon home demand, but can sell it services in

[7] In our example, before trade, (interest/rent) in France > (interest/rent) in Germany. The introduction of trade *reduces* the French ratio (interest falls, rent rises), *increases* the German ratio, and thereby brings them closer together than before. Under certain restrictive assumptions, the two ratios are exactly equalized.

the wider world market through exports of commodities requiring much of this abundant factor. Without trade, Australian land would have little value. The domestic population would have such a weak demand for wheat, wool, and other land-intensive products that much land might not even be cultivated or used for productive purposes. Land owners could not command much rent for agricultural land; wheat and wool prices would be low. With the introduction of trade, the situation would dramatically change. It would become profitable to rent the cheap and abundant Australian land to produce land-intensive products for the world market. The price of wheat in Australia would quickly rise to the world-market level (less transport cost); land would become valuable and rents would rise. Though trade, the abundant Australian land is made available to people in other countries where land is scarcer (and, therefore, more expensive). In this sense, trade evens out inequalities in factor endowments among nations. Trade serves as a substitute for factor movements that would *directly* equalize factor endowments.

A fourth effect of trade is its effect on world output—the gain from trade. We have already demonstrated that each country can obtain, through trade, combinations of commodities which lie beyond its capacity to produce at home. When each country specializes in those commodities in which it has a comparative advantage, world resources are used more efficiently, and world output is larger than in the absence of trade. In a world where human wants still outrun our ability to satisfy them, gain from trade through more efficient use of world resources is a powerful argument for trade among nations.

3

The Tariff Issue

Despite the strong logical case for free trade, many people do not accept it. Judging by the enormous literature on the tariff issue, it was ever thus! Books and pamphlets written about tariffs in the past 500 years would fill a good-sized library, but these volumes are extremely repetitious, and it is doubtful that a genuinely new argument has appeared in the past 200 years. However, this is not to say that all tariff arguments are without substance and merit. Indeed, the persistence of the issue is partly a result of certain elements of truth in tariff arguments and partly a result of the fact that, as in every great issue of public policy, complex social, political, moral, and even esthetic considerations combine with purely economic considerations. Our discussion of the tariff issue will focus on the economic aspects, but we must remember that noneconomic aspects may sometimes dominate.

In this chapter we shall be discussing tariffs, but the real issue is protection, of which the tariff is just one special form. Nations have devised a great many protectionist devices over the years, such as quotas, exchange controls, and legal and administrative rules that discriminate against (or increase the cost of) imported goods and services. The case for and against all these forms of protection is essentially the same as that for tariffs, on which we shall concentrate.

I. WHOSE INTEREST IS AT STAKE:
MINE, YOURS, OR OURS?

Every tariff is dear to the hearts of some specific group within the economy (and within the body politic!). If cuts in tariffs on oranges, bicycles, or textiles are proposed, vigorous opposition will come from orange growers, bicycle manufacturers, and the textile industry. The particular group that forms to defend a tariff will usually include workers in the affected industry and owners of resources employed in it, but it may also include many people who are affected only indirectly. Sometimes a city, state, or even a region of a country may have a strong interest in keeping a particular tariff or in preventing a cut in it. Such groups clearly wish to *prevent the effects of trade from taking place*. They correctly recognize that their individual interest may be harmed if the tariff is cut.

In their zeal to make out a case for free trade, economists sometimes fall into a trap, and attempt to persuade (for example) a cotton-textile manufacturer that *his firm* will be better off without a tariff. Many words have been wasted in this vain (and mistaken) attempt! We have seen that trade causes shifts in resources, increases the demand for abundant factors relative to scarce factors, and changes the profitability and prices of different goods. These changes are likely to be painful in the industry whose output is reduced. Plants may be forced to shut down: workers lose their jobs and find that they must learn a new skill or accept employment as common labor; the plant and machinery decrease in value, and owners lose much of the value of their investment; and property values in the entire community may suffer.

From a practical standpoint, the fact that cuts in tariff can wreak such injury upon particular groups is one of the main reasons why tariff cutting is a slow, difficult process in most countries. Individuals, hurt by a specific tariff cut, will fight fiercely to protect their positions and, in a democratic country, they may join with other groups who are threatened with tariff cuts to make a common cause for the retention of tariffs. The very fact that injury is concentrated upon a relatively small group tends to make that group strong, vociferous, and politically effective.

The argument that a tariff cut will harm a particular group within the economy is difficult to combat precisely because the *argument is valid and correct!* It is often very easy to prove that a tariff cut will injure a specific group of firms and workers.

Perhaps the most difficult practical aspect of the tariff controversy is that one must clearly distinguish between *individual interest* and the *national interest*. Specifically, one must admit that a tariff cut will injure a single group, but he must then go on to prove that this injury is more than offset by the benefits accruing to the rest of the population. To prove that benefits outweigh losses is sometimes difficult, but the essence of the proof is contained in our explanation of the gain from trade— the demonstration that through trade and specialization the country, as a whole, can obtain combinations of the two goods that lie beyond its capacity to produce with its own resources. The injured group can be compensated for the loss that it has suffered and, still, the community as a whole will be better off.

The tariff advocate usually seeks a wider justification for a tariff than narrow self-interest. Sometimes an injured group will say, "What is good for us is good for the country. Therefore, this tariff is good for the country." But most arguments for tariffs seek to prove that the national interest is enhanced, and they therefore come into direct conflict with the principle of comparative advantage.

The case for free trade is simple but powerful: any interference with trade reduces the scope for geographical specialization, causes resources to be allocated less efficiently than with free trade, and therefore reduces total world output and real income. Many ingenious arguments have been devised in an attempt to break the hard logic of the case for free trade, but few of them have made much of a dent in it. We shall briefly examine a few of the most durable arguments.

II. CHEAP FOREIGN LABOR

Money wages in the United States are considerably higher than wages in other countries. Our wages are two to four times as

Table 3-1. Average Wage Rates in Manufacturing—1968 (United States Dollars per Hour)

United States	$3.01
United Kingdom	1.27
Germany	1.19
France	.76
Mexico	.80
Japan	.92
India	.15

Source. United Nations, *Monthly Bulletin of Statistics.*

high as English, French, and German wages, and twenty times the Indian. Table 3-1 contains figures for average wage rates in manufacturing. "High United States wages make it impossible for United States producers to compete with the products of cheap foreign labor. Unless we erect tariff barriers to keep out such goods, our producers will be undersold, our wages will fall, and our standard of living will be dragged down." So runs the argument for tariffs to protect us against cheap foreign labor. Stated in these terms the argument is wholly fallacious, yet it is probably the most pervasive and politically potent argument now used in the United States in support of tariffs.

We saw above that comparative advantage depends only upon relative price differences. If relative prices differ, specialization and gainful two-way trade will occur. Foreign conditions of production make no difference. Whether their wages are high or low, whether production is done by men or by robots who receive no wage at all—it does not matter. All that matters is that the foreigner is willing to offer us certain products on more favorable terms than we can produce them at home, so that through specialization and exchange we obtain a larger total amount of goods than we could produce at home. In our Franco-German example, France wanted to swap its wheat for German steel whenever it could get more than 1 ton of steel for 1 ton of wheat. It made no difference to France whether Germany produced the steel with much labor, little labor, or no labor at all. It made no difference whether Germany was rich or poor. The sole consideration determining France's gain from trade was its ability to obtain steel through trade at less cost than it could be produced at home.

High wages are made possible by high productivity of labor. Labor productivity depends upon the skill, energy, and industry of the workers, and particularly upon the proportions in which the factors are combined in the productive process. When skilled and industrious workers have much capital equipment to work with, their productivity will be high, and costs per unit of output can be low even though wages are high. Consider, for example, a construction project in which 1,000,000 cubic yards of earth must be moved, for instance, to back-fill a power dam. In India, the contractor hires 10,000 workers at 60¢ per *day*, and they take 100 days to do the job, using tiny amounts of capital in the form of crude mattocks and wicker baskets (to carry earth). Total cost is $600,000, or 60¢ per cubic yard. In the United States, the contractor uses 20 bulldozers, 30 earth-movers, and hires 50 operators at $5 per *hour*. If they do the job in 30 days (probably less!), his labor cost is $60,000 (8 hours x $5 x 50 workers x 30 days) and perhaps $60,000 for wear and tear on his equipment, or a total cost of $120,000 (12¢ per cubic yard). Despite the high United States wage, the cost per thousand yards of earth moved is only $120 in the United States compared to $600 in India. (The reader may ask, "Why does not the Indian contractor also use earth-moving equipment?" The answer is that capital is a scarce factor in India, and its price is much higher than in the United States. Also, India will allocate its capital to those uses in which it is most essential—that is, those uses in which labor cannot be substituted for it. Earth-moving is one activity in which labor can be substituted for capital, even though the resulting cost per unit is high.)[1]

Low foreign wages reflect the greater abundance of labor, relative to other factors, than in the United States. Foreign producers will be able to use the cheaper labor to produce goods that *require* much labor at lower prices than we can match. The

---

[1] Actually India *is* using heavy earth-moving equipment (imported) on some of the large construction jobs. One reason is that foreign aid and foreign loans at low interest rates are available for these specific projects and such capital funds are not freely allocable to the most economic use within India; another is that such vast amounts of earth must be moved that it would take years to complete the work with labor-intensive methods. The time required cannot be shortened by adding more labor because of crowding at the site.

greater abundance of labor is the basis of their comparative advantage, and foreigners will undersell us in those lines of production. The flaw in the cheap-labor argument lies in its assertion (or implication) that foreigners may undersell us across the board—in all lines of production—and thus force our standard of living to decline. Foreigners should be eager to use the proceeds of their exports to buy from us the products of those industries in which we have a comparative advantage—products requiring relatively much of our abundant factors of production. In these lines of production our prices are lower than theirs, despite the wage-rate disparity.[2]

If the cheap-labor argument were valid, one would expect to find United States wages low in our export industries, whose products are in direct competition with the products of cheap labor in their own home markets, and United States wages high in our protected industries. In actual fact, however, we find the opposite! United States wages are highest in the various lines of machinery production—agricultural, electrical, construction, etc. —and it just such machinery that comprises our largest export category. United States firms can pay high wages, absorb transport costs and foreign tariffs, and still undersell foreign machinery producers in their own backyards. On the other hand, our wages are lowest in industries such as cotton textiles, bicycles, and carpets, where foreign competition is an ever-present threat to existing producers, and where many firms survive only with the aid of tariffs against imports.[3]

The grain of truth in the cheap-labor argument is that a particular group in the United States may certainly be harmed by import competition based on low money wages. When Japan installs modern plants to produce transistor radios, flashlights, or wire nails, her lower wages give her an advantage over existing United States producers who must either shift into other

---

[2] We are here ignoring the frictional and transitional problems associated with an imbalance in trade. This matter will be further discussed below, but it does not alter the essential point that a nation's standard of living is a function of the skill and industry of its population and the quantity and quality of its capital and natural resources.

[3] For more information about the relationship between wage rates and trade structures, see Irving Kravis, "Wages and Foreign Trade," *Review of Economics and Statistics,* February, 1956.

products or shut down. Sometimes it is difficult to shift quickly into other products, and United States firms go out of business, throwing their employees out of work and creating "distressed areas" in the United States. The injured persons blame their trouble on cheap foreign labor and, of course, they are correct in the sense that low foreign wages are an immediate cause of their displacement. From the standpoint of the *national* interest, the question is whether the gain to the entire nation exceeds the loss suffered by this particular group. If it does—as comparative advantage clearly indicates—then the nation should be able to compensate the injured group and thus reduce the inequity involved in forcing that group to bear the brunt of an economic adjustment whose benefits are widely dispersed. For precisely this reason, the Trade Expansion Act of 1962 contained provisions to extend "adjustment assistance" to firms and workers injured by tariff reductions.

Before leaving this subject, we mention that in the long run even the injured community or region may be better off to let the comparative-*disadvantage* industry go out of business. If it holds onto an inefficient, noncompetitive industry—one barely able to pay the minimum wage—it is asking for chronic trouble. The community might better abandon the declining industry to its fate and seek vigorous new comparative-advantage industries to take its place.

III. INFANT INDUSTRY PROTECTION

The advocate of tariffs to protect infant industries does not deny the validity of the principle of comparative advantage; he simply argues that when a new industry is started it needs some time to develop skills, learn new techniques, and increase efficiency so that it can reduce its cost per unit. He argues that, during the growing stage, fledgling firms in this infant industry must be protected from the large, efficient, established firms in other countries. Without such protection the new industry may be undersold and driven out of business before it has time to become efficient. The need for protection is only temporary, however. When the learning process is complete, and the infant firms have matured, they will be able to compete in world markets.

A *potential* comparative-advantage industry will have become an *actual* comparative-advantage industry; the tariff can be abolished.

Thus stated, the infant-industry argument is analytically correct. It does not conflict with the principle of comparative advantage. In terms of our earlier analysis of trade, the argument is that the country's *present* production possibility curve does not reflect its true potential. Given time to develop the infant industry, the production-possibility curve will *shift*, and the country's potential comparative advantage will be achieved.

This argument has great appeal for countries in an early stage of industrialization—countries eager to develop a modern industrial sector. They fear that their attempts to develop new industries will be defeated by vigorous price competition from already-established firms in advanced industrial countries such as the United States, Germany, and England. The infant-industry argument is now seldom used in the United States, but in our early history it was forcefully advanced by Alexander Hamilton in his *Report on Manufactures* (1791), and it was frequently used to support United States tariffs in the 19th century. Hamilton urged the necessity of tariff protection to shield the infant American industries from the ravages of competition with the then more-advanced industries of England and Europe. His brilliant and eloquent statement of the case makes remarkably fresh reading even today, but its application is primarily to underdeveloped countries. These countries frequently assert their need for protection against the giant industrial firms of the United States some of which have *net profits after tax* larger than the total national income of many underdeveloped countries.

Despite its analytical validity and its appeal to common sense, infant-industry protection encounters grave difficulties in actual practice. A country should use great care in extending such protection to its young industries. The crucial problem is that it is difficult to determine in advance just which industries possess a potential comparative advantage. If protection is extended to the wrong industry, the cost to society will be heavy. Firms will expand their capacity, but costs per unit will remain high, and continued protection will be necessary for their survival. Tariff protection involves a social cost in that consumers have to pay higher prices for the protected commodity than would be necessary with free trade. Such higher prices reflect the greater amount of scarce resources required to produce the commodity at home. If the industry develops a comparative advantage, the extra costs incurred during its infancy may be recovered during its maturity. But if a mistake is made, the nation is saddled with a continuing burden. The record is not clear, but infant industries have shown a distressing tendency to remain dependent upon protection. A mistake, once made, is not easily corrected. Owners and workers in the new industry have a vested interest in it, and they will fight to preserve it.

In view of the extreme difficulty of selecting the correct industries to protect, many economists argue that a country should let the market decide. They doubt that government officials, no matter how dedicated, honest, and intelligent, can have the wisdom and foresight to pick out, in advance, exactly those industries in which a potential comparative advantage exists. If an industry is potentially profitable, private entrepreneurs will discover it, and they will bear the cost of its learning stage just as they bear the cost of construction, capital equipment, and training labor in any new venture. Here, the issue is joined, as other economists argue that special incentives may be necessary to induce entrepreneurs to undertake the new venture, especially in underdeveloped countries where entrepreneurs are shy. Although disagreement exists, nearly everyone would agree that infant industry protection should be extended only when the country possesses an ample supply of the basic resources used in its production. With no coal or iron ore, Costa Rica would be unwise to impose a tariff on steel imports in the hope that an efficient, low-cost steel industry would spring up in response! Possession of an adequate supply of raw materials and natural resources thus seems to be a necessary condition for infant industry protection, but it may not be enough to assure efficient production and prices low enough to compete in world markets. When the protected home market is so small that it can support only one modern plant, there is no opportunity for a competitive struggle to determine which firms will survive. Everything depends upon the efficiency of the single plant. Even in the United States, 90% of new firms fail; thus the odds against success of an

infant firm are high in an underdeveloped country where entrepreneurs have many more unknown factors to cope with than
in the United States.

IV. TERMS OF TRADE

Free trade causes *world* output to be maximized, but the division
of world output among the trading countries depends upon the
exchange ratio between a nation's exports and imports—its terms
of trade. A single nation may be able to improve its terms of
trade and thus appropriate for itself a larger share of world
output. Economists generally acknowledge the *possibility* that a
single nation can benefit from a tariff at the expense of other
countries, but they do not consider that this exception to the
case for free trade has much practical importance, for the following two reasons.

First, the country imposing a tariff will benefit only if foreign
supply is less than perfectly elastic. (That is, the foreign producer
would reduce his price rather than sell a smaller quantity of his
product to the importing country.) For example, suppose that
the United States is importing tin at $1 per pound. If we put on a
tariff of $0.20 per pound, we might expect the price at home to
rise to $1.20 per pound. At that price, however, United States
users of tin might switch to aluminum. Rather than lose their
sales of tin in the United States market, foreign producers might
simply reduce their price (before tariff) to $.80, leaving the price
to United States users the same as before. In such a case, a
smaller amount of United States exports (wheat, machinery, etc.)
would exchange for the same amount of tin as before; our terms
of trade will have improved. In most cases we do not expect
foreign supply to be completely inelastic: foreign producers may
have other outlets for their exports, or they may prefer to shift to
other products, or they may prefer simply to reduce output. The
size of the country imposing the tariff is also important; the
smaller it is in relation to the world market, the smaller its
chances of improving its terms of trade. (Do you see why?)

Second, any benefit that a nation may obtain through improved terms of trade may be lost if the foreigner retaliates by imposing tariffs of his own. The situation might degenerate into a tariff war, in which total world trade is sharply reduced, the gains of specialization lost, and world output reduced. Everybody loses. Since it is unlikely that other nations would allow their terms of trade to be worsened without retaliating in kind, the analytical *possibility* that a tariff would benefit a single nation seems unimportant in practice.

V. NONECONOMIC ARGUMENTS FOR TARIFFS

Tariff protection is often sought as a means of attaining some objective that is desired for its own sake, where cost is not a primary consideration. For example, a particular industry may be thought essential to maintain a nation's military strength. Even though the industry is inefficient and its costs per unit are high, the nation may wish to pay the price and preserve its capacity to produce these essential goods. Similarly, the public may treasure some occupation or industry, such as glass blowing in West Virginia, small-scale fishing, or sheepherding, and may wish to preserve them to enrich the fabric of national life.

In all such cases the economist can only point out the cost of protection, and perhaps suggest alternative ways of achieving the same objective (such as subsidies to defense industries or to glass blowing firms). He cannot use economic analysis to prove that the objective is not a worthy one. Economists have always recognized this exception to the case for free trade, and even Adam Smith observed that "defense is more important than opulence."

Having admitted so much, we should note that it is extremely difficult to prove that an industry is essential for national defense.[4] Policy makers should cast a cool and skeptical eye on industry claims for protection on this basis, since producers of everything from garlic to clothespins have claimed it.

---

[4] *Defense Essentiality and Foreign Economic Policy: Case Study of the Watch Industry and Precision Skills.* Joint Economic Committee, July 18, 1956.

VI. OTHER TARIFF ARGUMENTS

Many other arguments have been advanced by tariff advocates.[5] Some of these are variants of the major arguments presented above. For example, advocacy of tariffs to achieve a more diversified economy may rest on the infant-industry argument or on the "noneconomic" argument that the fabric of national life is richer and more satisfying if a wide variety of production activities exists; even though variety costs more, it is thought to be worth the price. Thus one may support tariffs for hand-blown glassware so that tourists vacationing in Appalachia may visit such glass plants.

Some arguments derive what validity they have from imperfections in the economic system. For example, the popular argument that tariffs will increase domestic employment has most force when a nation is suffering from a high rate of unemployment. Higher tariffs *will* tend to increase employment in import-competing industries, although this gain will be offset when exports fall—as they must, either because foreigners retaliate by raising *their* tariffs or simply because their ability to buy our goods declines when we stop buying theirs. An all-round reduction in the volume of world trade simply robs the world of the fruits of specialization and the international division of labor. A French economist, Frédéric Bastiat, long ago demolished the argument for tariffs to create employment in a brilliant satirical essay, "Petition of the Candlemakers."[6]

Still other tariff arguments are wholly fallacious, although not less hardy on that account. These include the "scientific" or "fair-play" argument for tariffs "just high enough to equalize the costs of production at home and abroad, thereby enabling domestic and foreign producers to compete on an equal basis." Such tariffs would, of course, destroy the whole basis for trade by equalizing relative prices at home and abroad. While no one has seriously advocated a thorough-going application of this "prin-

---

[5] For an excellent detailed discussion of the numerous tariff arguments, see Lawrence W. Towle, *International Trade and Commercial Policy*, 2nd ed. (New York: Harper, 1956), Chs. 19–20.

[6] See Bastiat's *Economic Sophisms* (New York: Van Norstrand, 1964), or almost any volume of readings for introductory economics.

ciple," much solemn nonsense about the scientific tariff has been heard in United States political campaigns. Another such argument is that we "keep our money at home" when we buy domestic goods, and thereby benefit because we can "get the goods and keep our money too." The basic flaw in this argument is that it confuses wealth and money; it implies that a nation grows wealthy by accumulating a stock of money. Thus it fails to perceive the true nature of trade as an exchange of goods, with money serving only as a medium, and it therefore ignores the gain from trade arising from specialization. The argument is a survival from mercantilistic thought. Nevertheless, this crude fallacy, a hardy perennial sometimes attributed (falsely) to Abraham Lincoln, may be dusted off and made popular again now that the United States balance of payments is weak and the dollar is under pressure in world markets.

Most tariff arguments are fundamentally an expression of nationalism. The principle of free trade within a single nation is generally accepted, although regional conflicts do sometimes arise. But despite complaints in New England about textile firms moving to the South, or grumbles in the South about plant-location policies of large corporations, for the most part we accept the economic adjustments required by domestic free trade, technological change, and shifts in tastes. When the adjustment occurs because of foreign competition, however, we are much more likely to object. This difference in attitude came into sharp focus a few years ago when two neighboring Massachusetts towns were suffering from high rates of unemployment, one because a cotton textile firm had closed a local plant and moved to the South, the other because a watch manufacturer had reduced output and laid off workers because of competition from imported Swiss watches. Congressmen had difficulty justifying federal action (a tariff increase) to help the watch town at the same time that they urged the necessity for economic adjustment to the textile town. The same point is made in the following fable.

VII A FABLE OF TRADE AND TECHNOLOGY

During the middle decades of the twentieth century, an adventurous entrepreneur bought a thousand acres of the Great

Dismal Swamp in coastal North Carolina. After draining the land and building a road and rail spur, the mysterious entrepreneur, Mr. X., built a 12-ft. electrified fence around his entire property, posted guards at the gates, and allowed no one to enter except his own trusted employees. He advertised for workers, offering $3 per hour, and hired 5000 workers, all sworn to secrecy.

Mr. X announced that he had made several scientific discoveries and inventions which enabled him to transform coal, wheat, tobacco, petroleum, machinery, and other products into a variety of finished products, including textiles, cameras, watches, chemicals, and TV sets. Within a few months, vast quantities of materials were pouring into Mr. X's guarded compound from all parts of the country, and a flood of low-price industrial and consumer goods began to pour *out of* Mr. X's gates and into the nation's markets, where housewives and industrialists eagerly bought them at prices 20 to 30% below the competition. Mr. X's company, Consolidated Alchemy, Inc., (CAI) reported large profits, and was soon listed on the New York Stock Exchange where it became the growth stock of the century—a favorite of institutional investors.

Meantime, the nation hailed Mr. X as a genius and benefactor of mankind, a man whose inventions greatly increased the productivity of labor and improved the standard of living of the masses. He was favorably compared to Eli Whitney and Thomas Edison.

It is true that grumbles were heard in some quarters. Several manufacturers of TV sets tried to prevent their dealers from stocking or servicing CAI sets; textile manufacturers tried to persuade Congress to establish production quotas for each firm based on average output in the previous 50 years; a labor union picketed stores carrying CAI merchandise; and three New England legislatures passed laws requiring that stores display "Buy New England" posters. None of these activities had much effect, however. Buyers could not resist the low CAI prices, and many communities were prospering because of their rapidly increasing sales to Consolidated Alchemy. The Houses of Congress resounded with speeches calling upon the people to accept the necessity for economic adjustment and urging the benefits of technical change.

As for coastal North Carolina, it was booming as never before. Schools, houses, and roads were constructed; the Great Dismal Swamp was drained and used for truck gardens, its extraordinarily fertile land was selling for $3000 per acre; employment expanded, and average wages rose to $4 per hour.

Then, one Sunday morning, a small boy, vacationing with his family at a nearby seaside resort, tried out his new skin-diving equipment, penetrated Mr. X's underwater screen, and observed that Consolidated Alchemy's "factories" were nothing but warehouses and that its "secret technical process" was nothing but trade. Mr. X was, in fact, a hoax; his firm was nothing but a giant import-export business. He bought vast quantities of materials from United States producers, loaded them under cover of night onto a fleet of ships, and carried them off to foreign markets where he exchanged them for the variety of goods that he sold throughout the United States at such low prices.

When the boy told what he had seen, a wire service picked up the story, and within 24 hours Mr. X was denounced as a fraud, his operation was shut down, his thousands of high-paid workers were thrown out of work, and his company was bankrupt. Several Congressmen declared that the American standard of living had been protected from a serious threat of competition from cheap foreign labor, and urged higher appropriations for research in industrial technology.

4

World Monetary Arrangements

Different countries use different monies. With rare exceptions, each country has its own national currency.[1] Thus we have United States *dollars*, French *francs*, German *marks*, Japanese *yen*, and about 130 other national currencies. To make a payment from one country to another, we must arrange to convert one national currency into another because in the present stage of civilization we have not devised an *international* currency. This simple fact—that we must use national currencies for settling international payments—is the source of much difficulty and international friction. Nations, typically, regard creation and control of the national currency as a vital part of political sovereignty, and jealously resist any external interference with their sovereign power to control the currency. Friction, therefore, arises precisely because the practice of using national currencies to make international payments often affects the supply of money in the trading countries.

I. HOW INTERNATIONAL PAYMENTS ARE MADE

International payments are similar in most respects to domestic payments; the chief difference concerns the exchange rate. In

[1] We shall use "money" and "currency" interchangeably in this discussion. By currency we do not mean just paper money, but the unit in which a nation denominates its money. For example, the *franc* is the national currency of France, the *lira* that of Italy, the *dollar* that of the United States. The "supply of money" in a nation is the total amount of coin, paper money, and demand deposits denominated in the national currency unit.

Table 4-1.

	Chicago Bank
Assets	Liabilities
Reserve + $1,000,000	Meat-packer's balance + $1,000,000 (demand deposit)

	Boston Bank
Assets	Liabilities
Reserve − $1,000,000	Shoe factory's balance − $1,000,000 (demand deposit)

domestic commerce, most payments are made by check. People use coin and currency for small purchases, but individuals as well as business firms use checks for the overwhelming bulk of their payments. When a Boston shoe factory buys $1,000,000 worth of leather from a Chicago meat packer, it pays by check. The Boston firm's bank balance declines, the meat packer's bank balance rises, and the two firms let their banks worry about the rest of the transaction. Within the United States, what usually happens is that the check clears through the Federal Reserve System, which increases the Chicago bank's reserve and reduces the Boston bank's reserve. The net result is that bank balances (demand deposits) held by the public rise in Chicago, fall in Boston, but remain unchanged in total, while reserves shift from the Boston bank to the Chicago bank. This transaction appears in "T accounts" as shown in Table 4-1.

In international commerce, almost all payments are also made through the use of checks, drafts, or other financial instruments. The process is very similar to that just described for a domestic transaction, with the important difference that in an international transaction two or more national currencies are involved. Suppose our Boston shoe factory buys its leather from a French producer, agreeing to pay fr. 5,000,000 (equal to $1,000,000 when the exchange rate is $1 = fr. 5.00). As before, the Boston firm may pay by check, but now its dollar check must somehow be converted into francs.[2] Both the conversion and the

2 In actual practice, commercial drafts or bills of exchange are more often used than ordinary checks. However, the specific form of the instrument used does not affect the *process* that we are discussing. For a description of

Table 4-2.

United States Bank	
Assets	Liabilities
	Domestic demand deposits − $1,000,000 (Boston shoe factory) Due to French bank + $1,000,000

French Banks	
Assets	Liabilities
Due from U.S. Bank + fr. 5,000,000	Domestic demand deposits + fr. $5,000,000 (French leather producer)

clearing process are performed by commercial banks in the two countries. When the French producer receives the dollar check, he deposits it in a Paris bank and his account is credited with the franc equivalent of the dollar amount, that is, fr. 5,000,000. The Paris bank then sends the check to the New York bank with which it does business (its New York "correspondent"), and asks that the check be collected and credited to the Paris bank's balance (*in dollars*) in the New York bank. This is done in exactly the same way as in a domestic transaction. The net result of the international aspect of the transaction is that demand deposits held by the public rise in France and fall in the United States, and United States banks have increased their liabilities to French banks. This transaction appears in T accounts as shown in Table 4-2.

The French leather producer has received payment in francs; the Boston shoe firm has made payment in dollars. This international transaction has been made possible because commercial banks in the two countries are willing to hold balances with each other for clearing purposes. Commercial banks thus provide a connecting link between the two national currencies.

In the example just discussed, the French bank paid out francs (credited the leather producer's account for fr. 5,000,000) against a claim in dollars on the New York bank (a dollar deposit of $1,000,000). When Americans make payments to French in-

financial instruments used in international commerce, see Norman Crump, *The ABC of Foreign Exchange* (12th ed., London, 1956).

dividuals and firms, whether for French goods, tourist expenditures, villas on the Riviera, or French stocks and bonds, the flow of payments causes French commercial banks to build up larger and larger dollar balances in United States banks. On the other hand, when French citizens buy United States goods, services, and assets, the flow of payments causes French dollar balances to decline. If the two payments flows are equal in size in a given period of time, then the net dollar balances held by French banks remain unchanged. Commercial banks thus enable international transactions to take place; through their clearing operations, they make it possible to use national currencies (francs and dollars) as international money.

The reader may now ask, "What if things do not work out so nicely? What if United States payments to France exceed the payments from France to the United States—or vice-versa?" The answer is that either form of imbalance can be troublesome. Some of the most vexing issues in international finance are concerned with the arrangements that nations have made to deal with such unbalanced flows of payments. If United States payments to France exceed our receipts from France, French commercial banks will accumulate dollar balances in United States banks. At some point they will become unwilling to accept any more dollars. That means that French commercial banks will be unwilling to pay out any more francs for dollar checks unless they can exchange the dollar checks for *francs*. Under the present system, the Bank of France (the French central bank, analogous to the Federal Reserve System in the United States) may buy the unwanted dollars, paying for them in newly created francs. The Bank of France then accumulates dollar balances, but it also has a limit beyond which it will not wish to hold additional dollars. When that limit is reached, the Bank of France can use the unwanted dollar balance to buy gold from the United States Treasury, since the United States has agreed to sell gold to official buyers (such as foreign central banks and treasuries) at a fixed price of $35 per ounce.

On the other hand, if French payments to the United States exceed our payments to France, the dollar balances of French commercial banks will decline. (Work through the T-accounts to be sure that you see *why!*) If the French banks are to continue to perform the clearing function, their dollar balances must be replenished. Under the present system, the Bank of France can sell *its* dollar balances to French commercial banks in exchange for francs. If the Bank of France does not have any dollar balances, it can *sell* gold to the United States Treasury to get some.

The alert reader will have noticed that in our examples the French commercial banks had dollar balances in United States banks, but United States commercial banks did not have *franc* balances in French banks. The clearing process could of course be handled either way (or both ways), but in actual practice the process works approximately as we have described it. Foreign commercial banks customarily keep working balances in New York banks, and these balances are used for clearing payments to and from each foreign country.[3] This widespread practice is a reflection of the fact that the United States dollar is a "key currency" in international finance. Much trade is paid for in dollars even when the United States is not a party to the transaction. For example, a shipment of coffee from Brazil to Germany may be paid for by a dollar check, with the international payment accomplished by a transfer of dollar funds from a German commercial bank to a Brazilian commercial bank on the books of a New York bank. Such a transaction may appear as shown in Table 4-3 in the New York bank.

Table 4-3.

New York Bank	
Assets	Liabilities
	Due to German bank — $50,000 Due to Brazilian bank + 50,000

Corresponding transactions in each national currency—German marks and Brazilian cruzeiros—are made in each country.

In this way, national currencies are made to serve as international money. The great bulk of international payments are

---

[3] United States commercial banks do keep some working balances in foreign commercial banks, but these are ordinarily smaller than the balances that foreign banks keep with ours. Thus, the *net* position is as described above.

accomplished in approximately this manner, although in practice a great variety of complex details obscure the basically simple process. In the modern world, international payments are made by bookkeeping transfers on the books of commercial banks. Although the layman often thinks that gold is used to finance international transactions, its role is, in fact, largely limited to reserve adjustments made by central banks. (This does not mean that gold is unimportant, however. See Chapter 7.)

II. THE BALANCE OF PAYMENTS

The balance of payments is a summary record of all economic transactions between residents of one country (individuals, firms, and government agencies) and the rest of the world during a given period of time. Thus, it records the money value of the flow of merchandise between countries, purchases and sales of assets of all kinds, services bought and sold (such as shipping and insurance), and gifts made to or received from the rest of the world. All of the diverse economic transactions that cross a nation's borders are captured and summarized in its balance of payments.

Most transactions are settled in money in the manner already described, but whether a transaction involves a money payment or not, it is included in the balance of payments as long as a resident is dealing with someone in the outside world. If you send a food package to a child in India, or a watch to that girl that you met in France last summer, an economic transaction takes place between the United States and the rest of the world, and it should be included in the balance of payments.

Double-entry bookkeeping is used to record transactions in the balance of payments. For every transaction, *two* entries are made: a debit and a credit. If this rule is rigorously followed, total debits will always equal total credits. Such equality between total debits and credits has no economic significance, however; it simply results from the accounting procedure used. In order to use the balance of payments for economic analysis, we must classify debits and credits into economically significant categories. We can then compare the size of debits and credits in particular groups and attach economic significance to an excess of either of those groups. It is in this way that we shall define the terms "deficit" and "surplus" in the balance of payments.

But first: What do we mean by "debit" and "credit"? These elusive terms can best be defined by example, and by stating the types of transactions that give rise to each. We shall record a *debit* entry in the balance of payments to reflect any of the following.[4]

A. Goods and services acquired from foreigners.

B. Gifts made to foreigners (also called "unilateral transfers").

C. Long-term assets acquired from foreigners (or long-term liabilities reduced).

D. Short-term assets acquired from foreigners (or short-term liabilities reduced).

Similarly, we shall record a *credit* entry to reflect any one of the following.

A. Goods and services provided to foreigners.

B. Gifts received from foreigners.

C. Long-term assets given up (or long-term liabilities incurred).

D. Short-term assets given up (or short-term liabilities incurred).

By convention, monetary gold is treated as a short-term asset, and gold transactions are included in category *D*. That is, an export of monetary gold is a credit entry in *D* (short-term asset given up). Also, by convention, the distinction between short term and long term is, arbitrarily, set at one year. Any obligation (or claim) that falls due in less than a year is classified as short term. Bank deposits payable on demand are short-term deposits. Another useful convention to keep in mind is that balance-of-payments accountants treat debits as negative and credits as positive. Minus and plus signs are frequently used in published tables.

Every transaction falls into one of these four categories, and

---

[4] John Powelson, *Economic Accounting* (New York, 1955). See, especially, Chapters 21 and 22 for a thorough treatment of balance-of-payments accounting.

we have therefore provided both an operational definition of debits and credits and an exhaustive classification of items in the balance of payments. For example, we can compare debits and credits in category A, and see whether a nation buys more goods and services from the rest of the world than it sells. This balance of trade in goods and services, or "current-account balance," is one important measure of a nation's economic relation to the rest of the world. If a nation buys more goods and services than it sells (that is, it has a "debit balance on current account"), then it must pay for the excess purchases by selling off long-term assets (C) or short-term assets (D), by going into debt (C or D), or by receiving gifts (B). In our description of international transactions, we assumed that a United States purchase of goods from France resulted in an increase in United States deposit liabilities to French banks—that is, a credit to D. Analysis of the various categories in a nation's balance of payments yields many useful insights and permits an appraisal of its economic position vis-à-vis the outside world.

To illustrate the use of these definitions and classifications, consider the following sample transactions.

1. *A Japanese electrical utility buys steam turbines from an American manufacturer for $500,000; payment is made by reducing dollar deposits of Japanese banks.* The American firm is providing goods to foreigners; hence, one part of the entry is a *credit* under A for merchandise exports. The deposit liability of an American bank to Japanese banks has declined; hence the other part of the entry is a *debit* under D to reflect "short-term liabilities reduced." These entries are shown in Table 4-4, with each entry number indicated in parenthesis.

Payment in this case might be made by a dollar check drawn by the Japanese utility on its own bank balance in a New York bank, or the utility might instruct its bank to pay $500,000 to the American firm, reimbursing its bank in Japanese *yen*. Either way, Japanese-owned dollar deposits decline, which is a reduction in American short-term liabilities to foreigners.

2. *American firms buy $425,000 of coffee from Brazil, paying with dollar checks on New York banks.* The *debit* entry is under A to reflect goods acquired from foreigners. The *credit* entry is

Table 4-4.   Hypothetical Balance-of-Payments for the United States

Debit (−)		Credit (+)	
A. Goods and services acquired from foreigners		A. Goods and services provided to foreigners	
(2) Merchandise imports: coffee	$425,000	(1) Merchandise exports:	
(5) Tourist expenditures	30,000	Turbines	$500,000
		(4) Merchandise exports:	
B. Unilateral transfers (gifts) made		Wheat	75,000
(4) Government donation:			
Wheat to India	75,000		
C. Long-term capital			
(3) Assets acquired: Danish bonds	150,000		
D. Short-term capital and gold		D. Short-term capital and gold	
(1) Liability reduced: Bank deposit	500,000	(2) Liabilities increased:	
(6) Liability reduced: Bank deposit	25,000	Bank deposit	425,000
		(3) Liabilities increased:	
		Bank deposit	150,000
		(5) Liabilities increased:	
		Bank deposit	30,000
		(6) Gold export	25,000
Total debits	$1,205,000	Total credits	$1,205,000

under *D* (see Table 4-4). Brazilians now have larger dollar deposits in New York banks, which means that American short-term liabilities to foreigners have increased.

3. *The Government of Denmark sells a $150,000 issue of 20-year bonds in the New York capital market, adding the dollar proceeds to its foreign exchange reserves.* American buyers of these Danish bonds have acquired a long-term asset (or claim on foreigners), and the *debit* entry is therefore under *C*, long-term assets acquired. The *credit* entry is to "short-term liabilities increased," since Denmark now holds larger dollar deposits in the amount of $150,000.

4. *The United States Government donates $75,000 of wheat to India.* American wheat has been exported, so the *credit* entry is under *A*, for goods provided to foreigners. The United States has made a gift, or unilateral transfer, to India, so the *debit* entry is under *B*, gifts made to foreigners. Note that the act of making a gift is recorded as a debit, while the goods actually given are recorded as merchandise exports, a credit.

5. *American tourists travel in France, spending $30,000 for food, lodging, and amusements. They obtained the necessary francs by cashing dollar traveler's checks at French banks; the banks, in turn, added the dollar checks to their balances with New York banks.* The *debit* entry, under *A*, reflects the purchase of services from foreigners. The *credit* entry is to short-term liabilities, as United States deposit liabilities to foreigners have again been increased by these tourist expenditures.

6. *The Bank of England buys $25,000 of gold from the United States Treasury, paying with a check on its dollar deposit in a New York bank.* Since monetary gold is treated as a short-term asset, the export of gold is a "short-term asset given up," and the *credit* entry is under *D*. American deposit liabilities to foreigners have been reduced when the Bank of England draws on its dollar deposit, so the *debit* entry is also under *D*, to "short-term liability reduced."

We can now consolidate the entries recorded in Table 4-4, and construct a summary balance of payments for the United States. Note, particularly, that the several entries made in *D*—increases and decreases in United States short-term liabilities—can be offset against one another, leaving a *net change* in short-term liabilities. Most published balance-of-payments statements show only the net change in short-term assets and liabilities. Our summary statement is shown in Table 4-5. From this table we can see, at a glance, that the United States has an export surplus on current account (*A*); it sold more goods and services to the rest of the world than it bought. The United States has a debit balance of unilateral transfers (made more gifts than it received), and a debit balance of long-term capital (acquired foreign assets or made loans to foreigners). This debit balance of long-term capital can also be interpreted as an "outflow of long-term capital," or a "net export of long-term capital."

Table 4-5. Summary of Hypothetical Balance of Payment for the United States

Category	Debit (−)	Credit (+)
A. Goods and services	$455,000	$575,000
B. Unilateral transfers	75,000	
C. Long-term capital	150,000	
D. Short-term capital and gold		105,000
Total	$680,000	$680,000

If we consider the sum of $A + B + C$ in Table 4-5, we can say that the United States purchased goods, made gifts, and acquired foreign assets amounting to $680,000, while its sales to foreigners amounted to only $575,000. The difference, $105,000, was financed by a net increase in United States short-term liabilities to foreigners and by the sale of gold. (These two items are combined in Table 4-5.) We shall define the term "balance of payments deficit" to mean an excess of debits over credits in categories $A + B + C$ or, what is the same thing, an excess of credits over debits in category D. In this case, the United States debit balance on $A + B + C$ was $105,000, exactly equal to the net credit balance in D. A "balance of payments surplus" would be an excess of credits over debits in categories $A + B + C$, or an excess of debits over credits in category D.

Under this definition, when a country has a deficit in its balance of payments it is incurring short-term liabilities to foreigners or giving up short-term foreign assets (drawing down foreign-exchange reserves or selling gold), and when it has a surplus it is reducing short-term liabilities to foreigners or accumulating short-term foreign assets. Balance-of-payments buffs call our definition the "basic balance." They say that we have placed categories A, B, and C "above the line," and category D "below the line." Strange as it may seem, heated controversies rage among the experts about the proper place to draw the line, and about what items to put above or below it. Indeed, these controversies even have important implications for public policy.

To illustrate: consider the United States balance of payment for 1964, shown in Table 4-6.[5] Did the United States have a

[5] Even more detail is contained in the *Survey of Current Business,* June 1968. We have combined some of the accounts for brevity.

deficit and, if so, in what amount? Our fourfold classification gives one answer to this question. Table 4-7, part *A*, contains a condensed summary in our categories *A*, *B*, *C*, and *D*.[6] We observe that the United States had a net *credit* balance on *A* + *B* + *C* (therefore, a net debit balance on *D*) of $94 million. That is, under our definition the United States had a balance-of-payment surplus of $94 million in 1964.

Many economists, and especially the United States Department of Commerce, disagree with this measure of the United States deficit. They argue that some items in *C* should be put "below the line," and some items in *D* above it. Specifically, some critics say that: (1) increases in United States short-term assets abroad should be treated just like increases in United States long-term assets abroad because they are largely privately owned and are not part of the nation's official foreign-exchange reserves; (2) some United States long-term liabilities should be treated like short-term liabilities because they are payable to foreign central banks and governments and because the United States Treasury is simply engaging in "window dressing" when it persuades the foreign holder of short-term dollars to take a two-year "bond" (which is sometimes convertible into demand liabilities in any case); and (3) the "errors and omissions" term should be put above the line when it shows a net debit.

The adjustments called for by these critics would entail the following shifts between categories *C* and *D* in Table 4-7, part *A*.

1. On the debit side, United States private short-term capital ($2147 million) and errors and omissions (860 million) are shifted from *D* to *C*.

2. On the credit side, U.S. private short-term nonbank liabilities ($113 million) are shifted from *D* to *C*.

---

[6] We have put "errors and omissions" in *D*. This item arises because balance-of-payments accountants do not have full double-entry information about every transaction. They must estimate many items from independent statistical information, such as customs reports on the value of merchandise exports and imports, bank reports of changes in deposit liabilities to foreigners, and the like. The "errors and omissions" item is a residual—the difference between totals estimated independently for debits and credits.

Table 4-6. Balance of Payments of the United States for 1964 (Millions of Dollars)

	Debits	
Goods and Services		
Merchandise (excluding military)	$18,648	
Transportation	2,462	
Travel	2,211	
Miscellaneous services	1,035	
Military expenditures	2,876	
Income on investments	1,456	$28,688
Unilateral Transfers (Net)		
Private	617	
Government (excluding military)	2,167	2,784
Long-Term Capital		
Private		
U.S. direct investment abroad (net)	2,328	
U.S. purchase of foreign securities (net)	677	
Other U.S. long-term loans	1,426	
Government		
U.S. Government loans	2,394	6,825
Short-Term Capital and Gold		
U.S. private short-term loans, etc.	2,147	
U.S. acquisition of foreign convertible currencies	220	
Errors and omissions	860	3,227
Total		$41,524

Source. *Survey of Current Business*, June 1968.

These changes have the following effect on categories C and D as given in Table 4-7, part A:

		Debit	Credit
C.	Original amount	$ 6,825	$ 1,293
		+2,147	+ 113
		+ 860	
	Adjusted amount	$ 9,832	$ 1,406
D.	Original amount	$ 3,227	$ 3,133
		−2,147	− 113
		− 860	
	Adjusted amount	$ 220	$ 3,020

Credits

Goods and Services		
Merchandise (excluding military)	$25,299	
Transportation	2,324	
Travel	1,207	
Miscellaneous services	2,135	
Military transactions	747	
Income on investments	5,386	$37,098
Long-Term Capital		
Private		
Foreign direct investment in U.S. (net)	−5	
Foreign purchase of U.S. securities, and loans	115	
Government		
Repayment of U.S. Government loans	717	
U.S. Government liabilities associated with specific transactions	466	1,293
Short-Term Capital and Gold		
U.S. commercial and brokerage liabilities	113	
Short-term liabilities to foreign commercial banks and private	1,797	
Short-term liabilities to foreign central banks and governments	832	
Net U.S. position in IMF	266	
Gold export	125	3,133
Total		**$41,524**

Source. Survey of Current Business, June 1968.

When these changes are made, our summary statement of the United States balance of payments in Table 4-7, part *A*, is changed as shown in Table 4-7 part *B*. The surplus becomes a deficit of $2800 million. Thus, the effect of these adjustments is to convert a small United States surplus into a substantial deficit! This concept of the deficit is reported by the Department of Commerce as the "balance of liquidity basis."

Although the change in arrangement of the numbers does not change the actual circumstances, the difference in interpretation is, nevertheless, important because public confidence in the dollar and its standing in world finance may be greatly affected by official reports on the size of the deficit or surplus. Indeed, this matter became so important that a special committee was appointed by the President to study it. The committee recommended a com-

CAMROSE LUTHERAN COLLEGE
LIBRARY

Table 4-7. Summary Balance of Payments of the United States for 1964 (Millions of Dollars)

	Category	A Debit (−)	Credit (+)	Net
A.	Goods and services	$28,688	$37,098	+ $8,410
B.	Unilateral transfer (net)	2,784		− 2,784
C.	Long-term capital	6,825	1,293	− 5,532
	TOTAL, A + B + C	38,297	38,391	+ 94
D.	Short-term capital and gold	3,227	3,133	− 94
		41,524	41,524	0

	Category	B Debit (−)	Credit (+)	Net
A.	Goods and services	$28,688	$37,098	+8,410
B.	Unilateral transfer (net)	2,784		−2,784
C.	Long-term capital	9,832	1,406	−8,426
	TOTAL, A + B + C	41,304	38,504	−2,800
D.	Short-term capital and gold	220	3,020	+2,800
		$41,524	$41,524	0

Source. Table 4-6.

promise definition that yields deficits lying in between those that we obtained in Table 4-7. The major change is that the committee would move short-term liabilities to foreign commercial banks

Table 4-8. U.S. Balance of Payments Position for Three Definitions 1960–1967.[a] (Millions of Dollars)

Year	Basic Balance	Liquidity Basis	Official Reserve Transactions
1960	−1,568	− 3,901	− 3,403
1961	− 143	− 2,371	− 1,347
1962	− 547	− 2,204	− 2,702
1963	−1,618	− 2,670	− 2,011
1964	+ 94	− 2,800	− 1,564
1965	−1,921	− 1,335	− 1,289
1966	−1,022	− 1,357	+ 266
1967	−2,213	− 3,571	− 3,405
TOTAL 1960–1967 incl.	−8,938	−20,209	−15,455

Source. Survey of Current Business, June 1968.

[a] In this table a *minus* sign indicates a U.S. deficit, a *plus* sign a U.S. surplus.

and private holders from category D to C.[7] In 1964 this shift reduced the reported United States deficit by $1797 million and produced a measure of the deficit almost equivalent to the "balance on official reserve transactions basis" now also reported by the Department of Commerce.

All three of these concepts of balance-of-payments deficit or surplus are used, despite the fact that they yield widely varying measures of the U.S. payments' position. In most recent years, the U.S. deficit has been largest on the "liquidity basis" and smallest on the "basic balance" definitions. Exceptions do exist, however. Table 4-8 contains comparative figures for 1960 to 1967. For the entire eight-year period, the U.S. deficit was $20 billion on the "liquidity" definition, but only $9 billion on the "basic balance."

III. EXCHANGE RATES

An exchange rate is a price: the price of one currency in terms of another. It is an extremely important price because it connects the price *systems* of two different countries, thus enabling traders to compare prices directly. If, as someone has remarked, a foreigner's money seems as strange as his language, the exchange rate is like a one-word dictionary that can translate all prices from the foreign tongue into our own. Imagine that you have a British mail-order catalog, with all articles carrying prices stated in pounds, shillings, and pence, and you are trying to compare its prices with those in a Sears and Roebuck catalog. Each catalog contains thousands of articles, but when you know *one* additional price, namely the dollar-pound exchange rate, you can compare prices of all similar articles. Furthermore, when the exchange rate changes, all these price comparisons change— relative prices are all affected.

At present the dollar-pound rate is $2.40 = £1. If the pound were devalued so that $2 = £1, all British goods would immediately be cheaper in terms of dollars. For example, a woolen suit costing £20 would fall in price from $48 to $40; a pair of shoes costing £5 would fall from $12 to $10. (We assume that

[7] *The Balance of Payments Statistics: A Review and Appraisal.* Report of the Review Committee to the Bureau of the Budget, April 1965.

prices in *pounds* remain the same. In practice, devaluation may put upward pressure on British prices.) Similarly, the prices of all United States goods would increase in terms of pounds. To buy an American machine costing $240, the British buyer must pay £120 instead of £100. Changes in the exchange rate can, therefore, have a powerful effect on imports and exports of the countries concerned. In view of its importance, it is not surprising to find that governments have long taken a keen interest in the determination of exchange rates. We shall briefly examine two alternative methods for setting them: fixed exchange rates and fluctuating exchange rates.

A. *Fixed Exchange Rates*

Under the present system, based on the International Monetary Fund (IMF), each nation chooses a "par value" for its currency in terms of the United States dollar. The dollar is the centerpiece, the base to which all other currencies are linked.[8] Table 4-9 contains a few illustrative par values prevailing in 1969. Note that when every currency is linked to the dollar, an exchange value between any two other currencies is also implied. These implied exchange values are called "cross-rates." For example, when $2.40 = £1 and 1 Mexican peso = $0.08, we can readily calculate the par value of the pound in Mexican pesos (peso 30 = £1). (For practice, calculate the exchange rate between the pound and each other currency in Table 4-9.)

In the IMF system, nations undertake not only to set par values for their currencies but also to keep the actual market exchange rates within 1% above or below the official par. Our "fixed rates" are, therefore, held inside that narrow range around the par value, but are permitted to fluctuate within it. For example, the United Kingdom pound can vary from $2.382 to $2.418.[9]

---

[8] Technically, a country may link its currency unit to gold instead of to the dollar. For example, the United Kingdom pound is linked to gold at the fixed price of £14 7/12 = 1 oz. Since the United States dollar is linked to gold at $35 = 1 oz., we obtain a fixed "par value," $2.40 = £1.00 ($35 ÷ 14 7/12 = $2.40). The gold "link" is somewhat artificial, however, because no nation except the United States is actually willing to buy and sell gold at the stated price.

[9] Several nations, including the United Kingdom, voluntarily limit market

Table 4-9. Selected Par Values, 1969

Country	Currency	Par Value in U.S. Dollars	Units of Foreign Currency per U.S. Dollar
France	Franc	$0.18004	5.5542
Germany	Mark	0.2732	3.66
India	Rupee	0.1333	7.50
Italy	Lira	0.0016	625.000
Mexico	Peso	0.08	12.500
United Kingdom	Pound	2.40	0.417

Source. IMF, *International Financial Statistics*, Nov. 1969.

What keeps the actual market rate within this narrow range? The answer is that the government (or its agent, the central bank) must operate a "price-support" scheme. Just as the United States government can support the price of wheat at, for example, $2 per bushel by standing ready to buy all wheat offered at that price, so the United Kingdom can support the price of the pound at $2.38 by standing ready to buy pounds at that price. It prevents a rise in the price above $2.42 by *selling* pounds at that price.

The mechanism of support is very simple. When United Kingdom payments to the United States exceed United States payments to the United Kingdom, the dollar balances of London commercial banks will fall. (Americans are receiving pound checks, and New York banks are changing these against the dollar balances of London banks.) As their dollar balances fall, London banks tend to charge a higher price for dollars. They offer a lower price for the pound, for instance, reducing it from $2.40 to $2.39. (Exchange rates are tricky! Note, carefully, that a *fall* in the dollar price of the pound is the same thing as a *rise* in the pound price of the dollar.) As the London banks reduce their dollar price for the pound toward the support level, $2.38, the United Kingdom Exchange Stabilization Fund (an agent of the government) will begin to buy pounds, paying with checks drawn on its dollar balance. These dollars are then credited to the accounts of London banks in New York, thus inducing them to continue selling dollars to commercial customers at or above

fluctuations to the narrower range of three quarters of 1% above and below the official par.

the support price. Similarly, a rise in the value of the pound to $2.42 would be checked by sales of pounds by the United Kingdom Stabilization Fund. Such sales would reduce the dollar balances of London banks.

This process has a straightforward interpretation in terms of demand and supply. In Figure 4-1 we show the trade demand for pounds at various exchange rates in the demand curve *DD*. This curve indicates that at lower prices for the pound, larger amounts will be purchased by importers, tourists, and others who want to make payment to the United Kingdom. Similarly, the trade supply of pounds is represented by the supply curve *SS*. It shows the amounts of pounds that will be offered by English importers and other United Kingdom residents who want to make payments to the United States.

In the situation depicted in Figure 4-1, the supply of pounds

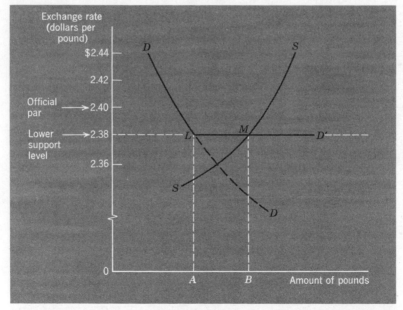

Figure 4-1. Dollar-pound exchange rate. The demand curve *DD* represents the amount of pounds that traders offer to buy at various exchange rates. The supply curve represents the amount of pounds that traders offer to sell at various exchange rates. At the official par value, supply exceeds demand, and the exchange rate falls. At $2.38 = £1, the lower support level, the United Kingdom Stabilization Fund buys all pounds not taken by private buyers, *LM*.

exceeds demand at the official par value, $2.40, and the price of the pound will fall. When the price reaches the lower support limit, $2.38, the United Kingdom Stabilization Fund begins to buy pounds. Its action makes the demand curve for pounds become perfectly elastic at the support price; that is, the effective demand curve in Figure 4-1 is the broken curve *DLD'*. The Stabilization Fund will buy *LM* (= *AB*) pounds, thus absorbing the excess supply at the support price. It pays for these pounds in dollars, which means that the support operation reduces official dollar holdings. Since United Kingdom dollar reserves are limited in amount, the Stabilization Fund cannot support the pound indefinitely.

The upper limit on the exchange rate is fixed in a similar way. If the demand for pounds exceeds supply at the official par value, the dollar price of the pound will rise. When it reaches the upper limit, for example $2.42, the Stabilization Fund begins to *sell*

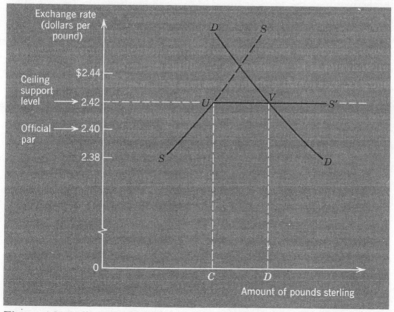

Figure 4-2. Dollar-pound exchange rate. The demand for pounds exceeds supply at the official part value, $2.40 = £1.00, hence the price of the pound rises. At the ceiling exchange rate, $2.42 = £1, the United Kingdom Stabilization Fund supplies pounds to satisfy the excess of demand over supply in the private market. Thus it sells *UV* (= *CD*) of pounds in this case.

pounds. Thus the supply curve becomes perfectly elastic at that price and the price cannot rise further. Figure 4-2 illustrates this situation; the effective supply curve is SUS'. The Stabilization Fund sells UV ($= CD$) of pounds at $2.42, thus satisfying the excess demand for pounds and increasing the Stabilization Fund's holding of dollars.

Through the operation of such a Stabilization Fund, the dollar-pound exchange rate can be held within the narrow range $2.38 to $2.42. A similar technique is used by other member nations of the IMF to keep the exchange rates for their currencies within 1% of their official par values. It can readily be seen that difficulties may arise whenever the Stabilization Fund must continuously buy (or continuously sell) the domestic currency. If it must continuously buy up an excess supply of domestic currency, it is in danger of exhausting its foreign-exchange reserves (dollar balances, in our case). If it must continuously sell domestic currency, it may build up an uncomfortably large holding of foreign-exchange reserves. It is, therefore, imperative that a fixed-exchange rate system contain some mechanism for correcting a situation of excess demand or excess supply. In terms of Figures 4-1 and 4-2, this means that it must be possible to bring about shifts in the demand and supply curves adequate to produce an exchange rate lying *within* the 1% range. We shall return to this matter in Chapter 7.

B. *Freely Fluctuating Exchange Rates*

As the name implies, a freely fluctuating exchange rate is one that is allowed to find its own level in the market. The government does not announce any official exchange rate for its currency unit, but allows the rate to move freely in the market. For any given demand-and-supply curves in the foreign-exchange market, the exchange rate moves to the level necessary to clear the market. For example, in Figure 4-3 with initial demand (D_1), and supply (S_1), the price of the pound will be $2.40. If the demand for pounds increases, for example, to D_2, the price of a pound rises to $3.50 in Figure 4-3.

The great virtue of this system is that external balance is continuously maintained by movements in exchange rates. At any given time the amount of foreign exchange demanded is

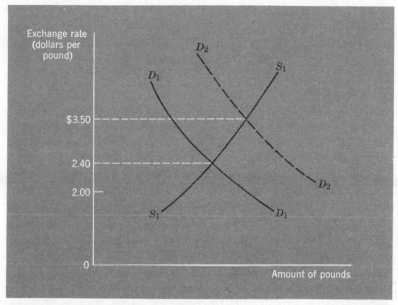

Figure 4-3. Exchange-rate determination under freely fluctuating system. With demand D_1 and supply S_1, the equilibrium exchange rate is $2.40 = £1. If demand shifts to D_2, the pound rises to $3.50, where it is again in equilibrium.

made equal to the amount supplied; any discrepancy is remedied by a change in the exchange rate. In this system, the government need not operate a Stabilization Fund to regulate the exchange rate, nor does it need to worry about the size of its foreign-exchange reserves.

Actions taken by the government will have effects on the demand and supply curves, however, and the government therefore has an influence on the level of the exchange rate. If the government increases its expenditures, financing them through central bank credit and thus creating inflationary pressures in the economy, it can expect the value of its currency to fall in the foreign exchange market. In Figure 4-3, for example, if the United Kingdom took such actions, the supply of pounds would increase (shift to the right) while the demand for pounds would fall (shift to the left). Both movements would drive down the dollar price of the pound.

At first glance, fluctuating exchange rates look like an easy and attractive solution for balance-of-payments problems. It is somewhat surprising, therefore, to find that fluctuating rates have rarely been used in the 20th century and that governments are almost unanimously hostile to them.[10] So is the banking community, for the most part.

An extensive literature exists on the advantages and disadvantages of fluctuating exchange rates. We shall briefly state three of the arguments against them. First, if elasticities of demand and supply of foreign exchange are very small, shifts in demand or supply will cause relatively large changes in exchange rates. Figure 4-4 illustrates this point. The shift in demand from D_1 to D_2 causes a large increase in the price of foreign exchange from P_1 to P_2. It is argued that large and frequent changes in exchange rates would disrupt trade. Furthermore, with given prices in each country, the exchange rate determines which commodities will be imported and exported. Large changes in the exchange rate change comparative advantage positions and call for resource movements, as explained in Chapter 2. Such changes in exchange rates, if frequent, could cause much wasteful movement of resources into and out of industries on the borderline of comparative advantage. On the other hand, if supply were elastic as indicated by S'_1 in Figure 4-4, the same shift in demand would cause only a small rise in the exchange rate.

Second, changes in an exchange rate are alleged to set in motion forces that will cause further changes in the same direction. That is, exchange rate changes are alleged to be cumulative and self-reinforcing. When the price of foreign exchange rises, we expect the prices of imports to rise in terms of domestic currency. If imported goods are an important item in the worker's family budget, the rise in his cost of living may lead to demands for higher wages. *If workers succeed in getting higher money wages,* prices and costs of production will rise; the demand for foreign exchange will rise because the workers, having larger incomes, will buy more foreign goods; and a further rise in the price of foreign exchange will take place. (Advocates of fluctuating rates

---

[10] Economists are divided on the merits of fluctuating exchange rates, but a considerable number of eminent economists advocate their use.

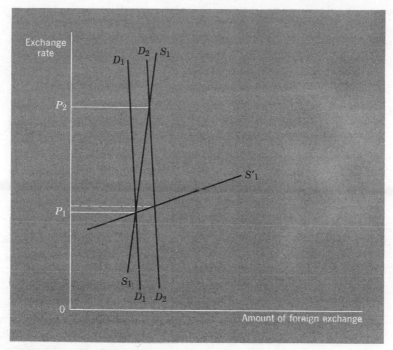

Figure 4-4. Low elasticities of supply and demand for foreign exchange cause large exchange-rate movements when demand shifts. In this case the shift in demand from D_1 to D_2 results in a relatively large movement in the exchange rate, from P_1 to P_2. If supply had been elastic (S'_1), the exchange rate movement would have been much smaller.

counter the argument by saying that wages should not be allowed to rise.)

The third argument is related to the second one. It is often maintained that speculation in foreign exchange will cause large and possibly cumulative movements in exchange rates. When the price of foreign exchange rises, speculators may guess that it will rise further. Therefore, they buy foreign exchange, and their added demand causes the price to rise. In such a case, the speculators, acting on the basis of their expectation of future exchange rate changes, actually cause those expectations to be realized. Therefore, it is argued, speculation will cause excessively large movements in exchange rates. These changes not only disrupt trade but also cause wasteful resource movements to occur. (Advocates deny that speculation will cause such large movements in exchange rates. They argue that speculation will tend to stabilize exchange rates, smoothing out and moderating the fluctuations that would otherwise occur.)

The controversy over fixed and fluctuating exchange rates is vigorous, heated, and extremely important, but it is largely an intellectual, even academic, debate. "Practical men" are almost solidly in favor of fixed exchange rates, or at least rates that change only rarely. Nearly all governments fix official par values for their currencies; indeed, the International Monetary Fund requires member nations to fix official par values and support them as we have described. The charter of the Fund does not even provide for the use of a fluctuating exchange rate. At the present time, no important country allows its currency to fluctuate freely. The Canadian dollar was allowed to "float" from 1950 to 1962, with only a small amount of government participation in the market to influence its level, but Canada returned to the IMF fold in 1962 when it fixed a par value of United States $0.92\frac{1}{2}$ = Can. $1.

Despite their unpopularity with bankers and treasury officials, fluctuating exchange rates may yet be used on a wider scale if nations continue to have difficulties making the fixed-exchange rate system work.

IV. THE INTERNATIONAL MONETARY FUND: A GOLD-EXCHANGE STANDARD

As we have seen, under the IMF each nation sets an official par value for its currency in terms of gold or the United States dollar, and keeps the market exchange rate within 1% of the par value by operating a Stabilization Fund. Thus, in the *short run*, exchange rates are fixed within this narrow range.

The founders of the International Monetary Fund realized that nations might be unable or unwilling to support a fixed exchange rate indefinitely. Therefore, the conferees at the Bretton Woods Conference in 1944 wrote in a provision in the charter to permit changes in the official par value of a currency. Article IV provides that, if a nation develops a chronic deficit in its balance of payments, and suffers a steady drain on its foreign exchange reserves, it may propose a change in its official par value. Technically, approval of the IMF is required (for a change of more than 10% from the initial par), and the IMF is supposed to satisfy itself that a "fundamental disequilibrium" exists in the member nation's balance of payments. However, it has proved impractical to follow this procedure. Since it is impossible to keep the proposed change secret, a nation cannot afford to wait for the IMF to study the matter and reach a decision. During the interim, rumors of an impending depreciation would reach the market, and heavy sales of the currency would occur. Such heavy sales could quickly exhaust the remaining exchange reserves. In practice, therefore, a change is decided upon by the member nation and the IMF is simply notified when the change becomes effective.

The IMF charter thus provides for *flexible* exchange rates in the long run. It combines fixed exchange rates in the short run with flexibility in the long run. This system of "managed flexibility," or the "adjustable peg," represents a compromise between fixed and fluctuating exchange rates. It grew out of experience between the wars (1919 to 1939) when nations became disenchanted with both fixed and fluctuating rates.

The founders of the IMF evidently expected (and intended) nations to make rather frequent use of the adjustable peg. They expected nations to give priority to internal economic objectives, especially full employment and growth. If, in the pursuit of these internal objectives, the balance of payments developed a chronic deficit, the exchange rate would be adjusted. Official support at the new level (through the Stabilization Fund) was supposed to eliminate the disturbing influence of speculation.

These matters have not worked out as the founders expected. Many nations, including the industrialized nations of the Atlantic Community, have been reluctant to change the official par values of their currencies. They cling to existing par values, defend them with all the stratagems and special arrangements that they can devise, and consent to a change only as a desperate, last-resort measure. In this group of countries, depreciation of a currency is regarded as a bitter defeat, and changes in par values have been rare since the 1949 adjustments. The Canadian dollar was a floating currency from 1950 to 1962; the French franc was depreciated in 1957 and 1958; and two currencies—the German mark and Dutch guilder—were appreciated by 5% in 1961. Otherwise, exchange rates in industrialized nations of the Atlantic Community (including Japan) remained fixed in the 18-year period 1949 to 1967.

This period of stability ended in November 1967 when the par value of the U.K. pound sterling was changed from $2.80 to $2.40, a depreciation of 15%. A few other nations quickly depreciated their currencies in order to maintain their relationship to the pound. In 1969, France was again forced by inflationary pressures to depreciate the franc, this time by 11%, while Germany, after resisting heavy speculative capital movements, again *appreciated* the mark, this time by 8.5%.

This remarkable record of stability in exchange rates has not been easy to achieve. Recurrent crises have occurred, with one country after another being threatened with exhaustion of its exchange reserves. However, nations have learned to help one another. Central banks extended credit to the nation whose currency was under pressure, and the International Monetary Fund has increased its financial resources and made these resources more easily accessible to deficit countries.

Critics of the IMF argue that the adjustable-peg system is the worst possible combination that we could have. When a currency is weak, the central bank (or Stabilization Fund) must support it by drawing down the nation's stock of foreign exchange reserves. As this stock dwindles, speculators will know that there is a chance of depreciation, but practically *no* risk of appreciation, of the currency. Therefore, speculators are presented with a "one-way bet"—a chance to gain but no risk of loss if they sell the currency in the exchange market. When they take this bet, they put more pressure on the weak currency and increase the chance that depreciation will be necessary. Large reserves may be required to withstand a speculative attack on a currency.

5

Trade Between Advanced and
Underdeveloped Countries

A striking feature of the modern world is its division into rich and poor or into what we shall call "advanced" and "underdeveloped" countries. Advanced countries are the *economically advanced countries* of Western Europe and North America, to which group Japan, Australia, and New Zealand are usually added. Underdeveloped countries include all the rest of the world, except that we are omitting the Soviet bloc from our consideration.[1]

Underdeveloped countries are poor. About 800 million people live in countries where the income per capita is less than $100;[2] another 400 million live in countries where the per capita income falls between $100 and $200; and about 400 million live in countries where the per capita income is between $200 and $600. In advanced countries, on the other hand, about 600 million people have per capita incomes ranging from $900 in Ireland to $4000

[1] The U.S.S.R., Poland, Czechoslovakia, and other East European countries might well be classed as "intermediate" if they were included, while Mainland China would be an underdeveloped country. Indeed, China constitutes about one third of the underdeveloped world in terms of population. However, we omit the Soviet bloc because the nature of bloc trade differs so greatly from that of the rest of the world.
[2] If Mainland China is included, 1.5 billion people fall into the under-$100 category, or almost one half of the world's population.

Table 5-1. Gross National Product per Capita, 1967

Country	Population[a] (Millions)	GNP per Capita[b] (U.S. Dollars)	
Underdeveloped Countries			
Bolivia	3.8	193	
Burma	25.8	70	
Ceylon	11.7	124	
Dominican Republic	3.9	280	
Ecuador	5.5	227	
El Salvador	3.2	283	
Ethiopia	23.1	64	(1966)
Ghana	8.1	216	
Guatemala	4.7	306	
India	498.7	64	(National income, 1966)
Iran	26.2	307	
Jordan	2.1	253	
Kenya	9.9	120	
Korea, Rep. of	29.8	150	
Malaysia	9.7	321	(1966)
Mexico	45.7	536	
Morocco	14.1	190	
Nigeria	59.7	75	(1966)
Pakistan	105.0	124	(1966)
Paraguay	2.2	228	
Peru	12.4	329	
Phillipines	34.7	199	
Taiwan	13.1	269	
Thailand	32.7	155	
Tunisia	4.6	220	
Turkey	32.7	295	(National income)
Uganda	7.9	86	
United Arab Republic	30.1	190	(1966)
Viet-Nam, Rep. of	16.1	147	(1965)
Advanced Countries			
Australia	11.8	2,296	
Austria	7.3	1,459	
Belgium	9.6	2,040	
Canada	20.4	2,856	
Denmark	4.8	2,332	

Table 5-1. (*Continued*)

Country	Population[a] (Millions)	GNP per Capita[b] (U.S. Dollars)
Finland	4.7	1,532
France	50.0	2,194
Germany		
(Federal Republic)	57.7	2,102
Ireland	2.9	916
Italy	52.4	1,274
Japan	100.0	1,154
Netherlands	12.6	1,801
New Zealand	2.7	1,682
Norway	3.8	2,231
Sweden	7.9	3,041
Switzerland	6.1	2,544
United Kingdom	55.1	1,709
United States	199.1	4,013

Source. Monthly Bulletin of Statistics, United Nations, February 1969.
[a] Population in 1967.
[b] Gross national product at market prices in national currencies, converted into United States dollars at the prevailing exchange rate, and divided by the population.

in the United States. Table 5-1 contains population and per capita income estimates for several countries.

These figures are very imperfect. The statistical difficulties of measuring money income in underdeveloped countries are enormous, and comparisons between countries present even greater problems. Nevertheless, the broad contrast that we have drawn is accurate enough—a contrast between a small group of relatively prosperous nations, mostly bordering the North Atlantic, and the rest of the world. In the underdeveloped world of Africa, Asia, and Latin America, only a few exceptions need be pointed out: Venezuela with its oil (per capita income $997 in 1967), Israel with its special advantages in a trained and educated labor force and foreign capital, and Japan with its amazing postwar growth that has moved it into our "advanced country" category.

It is true that considerable diversity exists within the underdeveloped world. For example, the difference between two under-developed countries such as Uganda and Mexico, or Indonesia and Turkey, may be greater than between an underdeveloped and an advanced country such as Mexico and Japan, or Turkey and Italy. Underdeveloped countries are poor, but some are certainly poorer than others. Some are in the process of building a modern society, while others are just emerging from feudalism or tribalism. Despite such diversity, it is still useful to classify countries into our two groups and to analyze trading relationships between them. For one thing, a sharp political cleavage between advanced and underdeveloped countries has emerged in recent years. Some countries consider themselves part of the underdeveloped club even though they have made considerable progress toward industrialization and have substantially increased per capita income.

An American finds it difficult to imagine what it means to live on an income of $100 *per year* (or $500 per year for a family of five).[3] After all, we have officially defined "poverty" in the United States to mean a family income of $3000 or less per year. It is, indeed, doubtful that a person could survive in the United States it his total income were only $100 per year. Yet the income statisticians solemnly tell us that millions of people live in countries where *average* income is less than that and, since we know that income is unequally distributed, most of these millions are living on far less than $100 per year. This comparison illustrates the weakness of our statistics of income and, especially, the hazards of comparing money income between countries. A farmer in Thailand may have no expenditures whatsoever for rent, heat, telephone, electricity, or water and only modest outlays for food, clothing, taxes, or insurance. He takes most of his food from field and stream, and he provides his own shelter. It is difficult to compare his income with that of an urban worker in the United States. Home production of food and clothing, rental value of owner-occupied houses, and other do-it-yourself items are *supposed* to be allowed for in national income statistics, but it seems doubtful that they are fully valued. Differences in prices in dif-

---

[3] For an attempt to convey this idea, see Robert Heilbroner, *The Great Ascent* (New York: Harper & Row, 1963), pp. 33–37.

ferent countries also bias comparisons. For example, rice costs 25¢ a pound in United States grocery stores, but 3¢ a pound (at the current exchange rate) in a Thai village. When rice is the staple diet, it makes a considerable difference which price is used to value the national product.

Even though we are skeptical of statistics revealing that per capita income in the United States ($4000) is 57 times as large as in Burma (70) or 53 times as large as in Nigeria ($75), it is certain that the disparity in income is very great. Whether the multiple is 57, 30, or 20 is not a crucial matter. What is crucial is that one half of the world's population still lives in grinding poverty. The nature of that poverty can be seen in many indicators of well-being other than money income: infant mortality, literacy, physicians per 100,000 population, consumption of electricity, life expectancy, incidence of various diseases, and many more.[4]

I. THE PATTERN OF TRADE

Ever since the Age of Exploration, the underdeveloped world has been engaged in trade with the more advanced industrial nations of the West. Indeed, the desire for trade was an important aspect of the outward thrust of European civilization from the 16th to the 19th centuries. Trade was a vehicle through which scientific advances, social change, and economic progress could be transmitted from leading to lagging regions and thereby disseminated throughout the world. In D. H. Robertson's phrase, trade was a marvelous "engine of growth."

In addition to its role as an agent of change, trade also increased income directly through the gains from specialization based on comparative advantage, as we have seen in Chapter 2. The clear conclusion, according to this traditional view, is that international trade stimulates and fosters economic development; hence, underdeveloped countries should adopt a policy of free trade and specialize in those lines of production in which they have a comparative advantage.

[4] See Stephen Enke, *Economics for Development* (Englewood Cliffs: Prentice-Hall, 1963), Chapters 2-3, for an account of the many dimensions of poverty.

Although trade was never fully free of tariffs and other restrictions, most of the underdeveloped countries did engage in active trade with industrial countries, and they still do. They specialized in primary products (food and raw materials), exporting these in exchange for a wide variety of manufactured goods. Thus, a pattern of trade developed between the two broad groups of countries. Despite this active trade and the close economic intercourse between advanced and underdeveloped countries, the income gap between the two groups steadily widened. The actual level of economic well-being in 1750 was probably not much, if any, higher in Europe than in China or India. Indeed, the early travelers from the West were dazzled by the wealth of the Orient! During the 19th and 20th centuries, the income gap steadily widened and underdeveloped countries began to suspect that the benefits of trade were unequally divided and that "free trade" was a clever Western ruse to keep them in a subordinate position. This suspicion and hostility toward trade became intermingled with attitudes toward colonialism and economic exploitation. One of the legacies of the fight against colonialism is a continuing suspicion that trade and other forms of economic intercourse may operate to the disadvantage of underdeveloped countries.

A. *The Network of Trade*

Dividing the world between advanced countries (A) and underdeveloped countries (U), we find that the major flow of trade is among the A countries themselves. A smaller but still very large amount of trade flows between A and U, but only a small amount of trade takes place among the U countries themselves. Table 5.2 contains actual figures for 1967. We see that trade among U countries amounted to only $8.1 billion, or 4.6% of total trade, while trade among A countries amounted to $110.2 billion (62%), and trade *between* A and U countries amounted to $58.7 billion (33.6%). It is clear that U countries do not trade very much among themselves. Their exports go largely to A countries, and their imports come from A countries.[5]

---

[5] Remember that we are omitting trade with the Soviet bloc. Such trade is quite small, however. In 1967, U countries exported $2.2 billion to the Soviet bloc and imported $3.3 billion—only 9% of their trade with A countries.

Table 5-2. Trade Within and Between Advanced and Underdeveloped Countries, 1967 (Billions of Dollars)

Exports[a] from	Imports of		
	A Countries[b]	U Countries[b]	Total
Advanced Countries			
Primary products[c]	30.8	6.0	36.8
Manufactures	79.4	23.5	102.9
Total	110.2	29.5	139.7
Underdeveloped Countries			
Primary products	23.6	5.9	29.5
Manufactures	5.6	2.2	7.8
Total	29.2	8.1	37.3
Total			
Primary Products	54.4	11.9	66.3
Manufactures	85.0	25.7	110.7
	139.4	37.6	177.0

Source. United Nations, *Monthly Bulletin of Statistics*, March 1969.
[a] Exports are valued F.O.B.
[b] A Countries include Western Europe, North America, Japan, Australia and New Zealand. U countries include the rest of the world outside the Soviet bloc.
[c] Primary products are categories 0, 1, 2, 3, and 4 in the Standard International Trade Classification.

B. *The Composition of Trade*

When merchandise trade is divided into primary products and manufactures, we find that U-country exports consist largely of primary products and U-country imports consist largely of manufactures. Table 5-2 also shows this division. U countries exported $29.2 billion to A countries, of which $23.6 billion was made up of primary products and only $5.6 billion of manufactures. (One half of these "manufactures" consisted of semiprocessed base metals.) On the other hand, U-country imports from A countries included $23.5 billion of manufactures and only $6.0 billion of primary products. (Of these primary product imports, $4.0 billion consisted of food.)

Primary products are also dominant in trade among U countries. Three quarters of such trade in 1967 consisted of primary products.

Table 5-3. Matrix of Trade in Engineering Products, 1966[a, b] (Billions of dollars)

Exports from	Imports of		
	A Countries	U Countries	Total
A Countries	35.1	12.0	47.1
U Countries	0.2	0.3	0.5
Total	35.3	12.3	47.6

Source. GATT, *International Trade, 1967* (Geneva, 1968), pp. 33-38.

[a] Engineering products include machinery and transport equipment (SITC section 7); scientific, medical, optical, measuring, and controlling instruments (SITC group 861); watches and clocks (SITC group 864); and miscellaneous manufactures of metal (SITC division 69).

[b] Countries included in each group are the same as in Table 5-2.

These trade patterns have existed for a long time. Similar estimates have been made for 1913, 1928, 1938, and for many recent years. The general pattern is the same. If anything, the contrasts are sharpening; trade among A countries is rising faster than the other categories. From 1960 to 1967, for example, trade among A countries doubled, while trade between A and U countries rose only 40%, and trade among U countries rose only 30%. It is a striking fact that the greatest expansion of trade has occurred among the industrial nations whose economies have been growing more similar.

It is also significant that the degree of U-country specialization in primary products has not lessened. Despite their efforts to diversify and develop manufacturing industries, U-country exports remain almost wholly concentrated in primary products. These countries are increasingly dissatisfied with the role assigned to them by the world trading system.

The virtual exclusion of U countries from export trade in products of technologically advanced industries is dramatically revealed in the data on trade in "engineering products." Table 5-3 contains the relevant figures for 1966. Of total exports of $47.6 billion of such products, A countries exported $47.1 billion (99%), U countries only $0.5 billion (1%).

C. *Concentration of Export Trade*

Exports of U countries are highly concentrated. In 45 countries, a single product accounts for over one half of the total exports.

In 55 countries, three principal products account for 75%, or more, of the total exports. See Table 5-4 for a tabulation indicating the dependence of countries on certain exports. Of the 55 countries depending on 3 principal exports for over 75% of their export proceeds, not one is an A country.

D. *Instability of Export Proceeds*

It is often argued that such a high degree of export concentration in U countries makes these countries vulnerable to fluctuations in market prices and in supply. A fall in demand—or a poor crop— can cause a large drop in export proceeds. Since exports generate a large part of national income in many U countries, big changes in export proceeds are a major disruptive influence in their domestic economies.

An influential United Nations' study[6] presented data showing that, from 1900 to 1950, the export proceeds of underdeveloped countries were highly unstable. For 18 major commodities, the average fluctuation from one year to another was 22%, up or down. For rubber alone, it was 36%. In the same period, the average change in price from one year to another was 14.5% for 22 major commodities. Instability of prices and export proceeds has lessened in recent years, but it is still great for individual commodities and for the countries dependent upon them. Figure 5-1 shows the behavior of coffee and rubber prices (monthly averages) from 1949 to 1968. Since coffee is the major export of several Latin American countries, these big changes in price have powerful political effects.

This view has recently been challenged by several writers, and especially by Alasdair MacBean.[7] MacBean's statistical investigations reveal no *general tendency* for U countries to experience greater instability in export prices and proceeds than A countries, although he acknowledges that individual U countries may suffer from an abnormally high degree of instability. MacBean also found no evidence of a general tendency for primary products to be more unstable than manufactured goods.

[6] *Instability in Export Markets of Underdeveloped Countries* (New York: United Nations, 1952).
[7] Alasdair MacBean, *Export Instability and Economic Development* (Cambridge: Harvard University Press, 1966).

Table 5-4. Concentration of Exports in Underdeveloped Countries: Percentage of Total Exports Accounted for by Three Principal Products, 1966

Country	Percentage	Principal Export Commodities
Bolivia (1965)	76.7	Tin, antimony, silver
Burma (1962)	75.8	Rice, oil-seeds, teak
Cambodia	82.6	Rubber, rice, corn
Central African Rep.	91.9	Diamonds, coffee, cotton
Ceylon	87.8	Tea, rubber, coconuts
Chad	90.3	Cotton, cattle, meat
Columbia	82.7	Coffee, petroleum, fruit
Congo (Brazzaville)	96.1	Timber, diamonds
Dominican Republic	75.0	Sugar, coffee, cocoa
Ecuador	84.1	Fruit, coffee, cocoa
Ethiopia	80.0	Coffee, hides, pulses
Fiji	86.0	Sugar coconuts, timber
Gabon	77.8	Manganese, wood, petroleum
Gambia	97.1	Vegetable oil, peanuts, fodder
Guyana	82.7	Bauxite, sugar, rice
Iran	90.2	Petroleum and products, cotton
Iraq (1965)	96.8	Petroleum, dates
Ivory Coast	79.1	Coffee, cocoa, wood
Jordan	76.0	Phosphates, vegetables, fruit
Liberia (1963)	94.5	Iron ore, rubber, gems
Libya	99.8	Petroleum, hides, peanuts
Malawai	77.8	Tobacco, tea, peanuts
Malaysia	77.5	Rubber, tin, petroleum
Mauritius	99.6	Suger, tea, copra
Niger	81.0	Peanuts, cattle
Panama	90.0	Fruit, petroleum, fish
Saudi Arabia	90.2	Petroleum and products
Senegal	78.2	Peanuts, phosphates
Sierra Leone	86.2	Diamonds, iron ore, palm
Somalia	83.3	Fruits, cattle, hides
South Vietnam (1965)	82.8	Rubber, tea, peanuts
Sudan	81.9	Cotton, oil seeds, gum
Togo	83.1	Phosphates, coffee, cocoa
Uganda	84.7	Coffee, cotton, copper
Venezuela	97.3	Petroleum and products, iron ore
Zambia	96.6	Copper, zinc, lead
Zanzibar	91.6	Cloves, copra, coir

Source. United Nations, *Yearbook of Trade Statistics, 1966.*

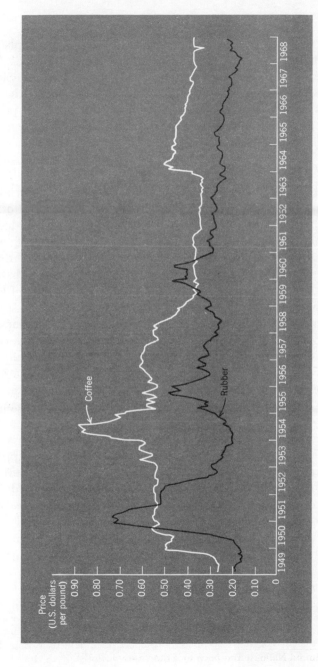

Figure 5-1. Monthly averages of coffee and rubber prices from 1949 to 1968. The range of fluctuation in daily prices is much greater than in these monthly averages. (*Source. International Financial Statistics*, International Monetary Fund.)

These new studies thus challenge one of the major complaints of U countries about the present system of world trade. So far, however, the new studies have not affected policy discussions very much. These are still dominated by the older view that U countries suffer from a high degree of instability in export prices and proceeds. U countries believe the cards are stacked against them in international trade.

E. *The Terms of Trade*

The final characteristic of trade between A and U countries is even more difficult to establish than the previous four. It is often argued that the terms of trade have turned against underdeveloped countries during the last 100 years—that the prices of their exports relative to the prices of their imports have declined.[8] Such a long-run decline in their terms of trade would mean that U countries were receiving a smaller and smaller amount of imported goods for a given volume of exports.

Hundreds of economists and statisticians have made millions of calculations, but they are still unable to settle this matter conclusively. The difficulties are conceptual, not just computational, so bigger and faster computers will not necessarily permit a definite answer. One major problem is that proper allowance cannot be made in the price indexes for new products and for changes in quality. Since these changes affect the imports of U countries more than their exports, to omit them is to exaggerate the rise in import prices and thus make the index of terms of trade appear less favorable than it should be. For example, a country exporting coffee and importing adding machines may find that each adding machine in 1969 can do 10 times as much work as a 1920 model. Therefore, if the price of adding machines has risen twice as much as the price of coffee, the terms of trade are highly favorable to the coffee exporter even though the statistical computation would show the opposite.

Another major problem is that changes in the commodity terms

[8] We refer to the commodity terms of trade, defined as index of export prices ÷ index of import prices. For example, from 1958 to 1963, Brazil's export price index fell from 100 to 83, her import price index rose from 100 to 104; the Brazilian terms of trade therefore declined from 100 to 80 (=83/104).

of trade do not necessarily indicate whether a country's *welfare* has improved. To determine the effect on welfare, a much more complicated calculation is required: one that can take account of changes in productivity of labor and other factors. This point can best be illustrated by reference to the problem of "fair prices" for the farmer, or what we call "parity prices." The parity-price ratio compares the prices that farmers receive with the prices that they pay, and is therefore the same thing as the commodity terms of trade. However, we recognize that improvements in machinery, seeds, fertilizers, and insecticides make it possible for a farmer to produce several times as much output (for instance, wheat) as he could produce with the same land and labor in the years 1910 to 1914. Therefore, even if the parity ratio is well below 100 (the terms of trade have turned against agriculture), the farmer is far better off than he was in the years 1910 to 1914. Exactly the same problem exists when we calculate the terms of trade of primary-producing countries and try to use the trend in the terms of trade as an indicator of the benefits derived from trade.

Other difficulties concern the methods to be used in weighting the commodities included in the index, methods of valuing imports and exports,[9] and choice of the base year.

Despite all of these statistical and conceptual problems, spokesmen for underdeveloped countries are firmly convinced that there is a chronic tendency for their terms of trade to worsen. They also believe that the adverse terms of trade are harmful to their economies, and that most or all of the "gains from trade" have accrued to advanced countries.

In recent years, especially since the underdeveloped countries have won their independence, they have challenged with increasing vehemence the traditional view of the beneficence of trade. They are profoundly skeptical and suspicious of trade and of the working of the world market system. They no longer accept

[9] Treatment of shipping charges makes a substantial difference. Much of the long-term deterioration in U-country terms of trade disappears when allowance is made for the great reduction in ocean transport rates from 1870 to 1900. See P. T. Ellsworth, "The Terms of Trade between Primary Producing and Industrial Countries," *Inter-American Economic Affairs*, Summer 1956.

the pattern of specialization and trade that seems indicated by the market, and their search for a "new trade policy" has become a crucially important issue in world affairs.

II. THE POOR COUNTRIES' VIEW OF THE FUTURE

Underdeveloped countries are pessimistic about the future role of trade, just as they are disgruntled about the way that it has served them in the past. Their case is not wholly logical, but it is, nevertheless, strongly and widely held. Indeed, this case has become so widely accepted among spokesmen for underdeveloped countries that we can speak of a "new orthodoxy." When 80 nations base their actions and policies on a particular set of beliefs, those beliefs are important whether correct or not.

The prevailing view of the prospects of trade, as seen by underdeveloped countries, can be stated briefly. They believe that their imports must increase, but that their traditional exports cannot increase at the same rate; hence they absolutely must develop some new exports to fill the gap. The new exports will run into competition in A-country markets, and access to those markets becomes a critical factor. Now we shall discuss each point in this capsule summary in more detail.

First, underdeveloped countries expect their imports to increase steadily. They hope to increase gross national product by 5% per year, and if they succeed, their imports will rise about 6% per year. By 1980, imports would reach $80 billion, an increase of $42 billion over 1967. An increase of this magnitude will be required to cover essential development needs. This calculation thus rests on the assumption that imports will be limited to capital goods, fuels and raw materials, plus some essential consumer goods. To keep imports to this figure, U countries must control their composition by tariffs, quotas, and other restrictive measures, thus limiting imports to those goods deemed essential to their development programs.

Second, underdeveloped countries doubt their ability to increase the value of their traditional exports of primary products— food and raw materials—as fast as imports will increase. They believe that the demand for these products in advanced countries is inelastic and growing very slowly, so that if they attempt to sell a larger quantity they will simply run into falling prices. Several reasons are given for the alleged slow rate of growth in demand for primary products. Rich countries tend to spend a smaller and smaller part of each extra dollar of income on food. The structure of production in rich countries shifts toward services and the more complex manufactures, with the result that raw materials comprise a smaller share of total product. Advancing technology tends to displace traditional raw materials with synthetics and manufactured substitutes. The remarkable development of plastics, synthetic rubber, and synthetic fibers are examples of such technological displacement.[10] Furthermore, advanced countries have made rapid technological progress in agriculture. They have expanded their own production of primary products, often with the aid of tariffs and quotas, and have thereby displaced imports.

Third, the new orthodoxy thus concludes that an alarming gap looms between the import requirements of underdeveloped countries and their prospective exports of traditional goods. Raúl Prebisch, a leading spokesman for U countries, has estimated that imports must rise at an annual rate of 6%, while traditional exports might rise only 2%.[11] On that basis, the trade gap by 1980 would be about $32 billion, as indicated in Figure 5-2. U countries must find $32 billion of additional exports or face the bitter necessity of cutting back their target rates of growth in income. Economic aid and other forms of capital transfer from A countries to U countries could also serve to bridge this gap, but our emphasis is upon trade itself.

Fourth, it follows that underdeveloped countries can no longer accept the proposition that they should specialize in primary production just because they have traditionally had a comparative advantage in such products. They must develop some *new* ex-

---

[10] Chemists are now trying to determine the chemical composition of the coffee aroma. If they succeed in developing a cheap substitute with the taste and aroma of real coffee, the economic impact on coffee exporters in Africa and Latin America would be enormous.

[11] During the 1950s, the *volume* of traditional exports rose 4% per year, but declining terms of trade reduced the rise in real value to about 2%. *Towards a New Trade Policy for Development* (New York: United Nations, 1964), p. 4. Prebisch was the principal author of this document.

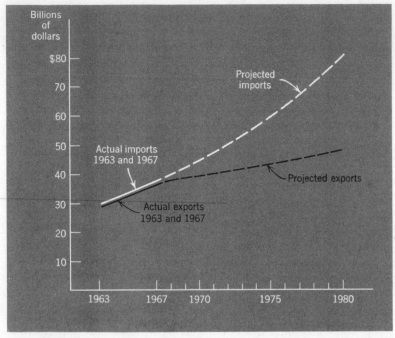

Figure 5-2. Actual and projected trade of underdeveloped countries. Imports are projected to increase 6% per year and traditional exports are projected to increase 2% per year, leaving a trade gap (excess of imports over exports) that reaches $32 billion by 1980.

ports to sell to advanced countries in exchange for the essential imports of capital goods. These new export products must include manufactured goods, and underdeveloped countries must demonstrate that they can expand capacity, produce efficiently, and develop a comparative advantage in some lines of manufacturing production. It is also argued, hopefully but without real proof, that U countries do have resources and a potential capability to develop new lines of production at competitive prices. If they can train labor, adapt modern techniques to suit their other resources, invest wisely in new plants, and foster entrepreneurial and managerial talent, their new industries may be able to emerge from the shelter of domestic protection and face the rigors of a competitive market. These are large "ifs," but they indicate the magnitude of the difficulties.

Finally, advanced countries must demonstrate their willingness to accept a rising volume of imported manufactures from the underdeveloped world. They must keep their markets open and show that they really believe in the market system. If they react to competition by raising tariffs and otherwise closing their markets to U-country exports, they will make it impossible for U countries to buy the imports that are vital to their economic development. U countries will then be forced to abandon the attempt to utilize the world market; they will be driven to the more arduous and painful path of building up their own capital-goods industries, either individually or in some kind of coalition.

Although this "new orthodoxy" is pessimistic about the prospects for expanding trade along its *present* patterns, it is cautiously optimistic and hopeful that a new basis for expanding trade can be found. Underdeveloped countries expect to continue to export primary products in about their present volume; there is no quarrel with the allocation of *existing* resources. The exchange of primary products for capital goods can continue to benefit both trading partners. The crucial issue for the future concerns the proper allocation of *new* capacity. U countries believe that, for the reasons we have stated, fresh additions to their productive capacity should go into manufacturing industries rather than into further expansion of traditional primary product exports. They argue that "incremental comparative advantage" differs sharply from the historical position. This point can be explained in terms of the theory of comparative advantage set forth in Chapter 2. At the present time, given their existing productive capacity, U countries have a comparative advantage in primary products. In Figure 5-3, the curve *AB* represents the existing production-possibility curve for U countries. With a world price ratio (terms of trade) between primary products and manufactures equal to the slope of the line *TT*, U countries produce at the point *P*, and trade *RP* of primary products for *RC* of manufactures. Through trade they reach a consumption point, *C*, which lies beyond their own productive capacity. This trade is extremely beneficial to them because they obtain much-needed manufactured goods.

If U countries now increase their productive capacity, putting additional labor and capital into primary production, their pro-

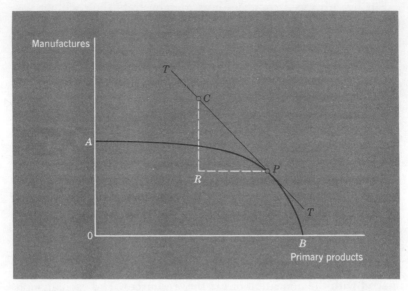

Figure 5-3. Present trading position of underdeveloped countries. The production possibility curve *AB* shows the various combinations of manufactures and primary products that U countries can produce with existing resources. Given the opportunity to trade with A countries at an exchange ratio equal to the slope of *TT*, U countries produce at *P*, and export *PR* of primary products to buy *RC* of manufactures. They consume the combination indicated by the point *C*.

duction-possibility curve will shift from *AB* to a new position such as *AD* in Figure 5-4. When they attempt to sell larger quantities of primary products on the world market, prices will fall and the terms of trade will turn against primary products, shifting, for example, from *TT* to *ZZ* in Figure 5-4. U countries will now produce at *Q*, but the increased volume of exports will not buy as much manufactures as before because the terms of trade have deteriorated so much. If they have already made the investments required to shift the production transformation curve from *AB* to *AD*, U countries will still be better off to trade than not to trade. Having incurred the sunk costs of expansion, they stand to gain from trade. But when we compare their positions before and after expansion, we find that they are not much better off—indeed,

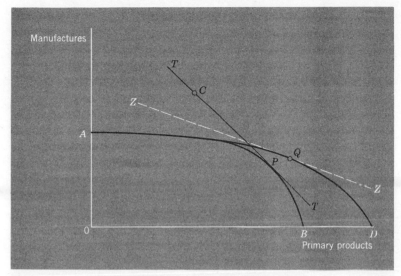

Figure 5-4. Expansion of capacity to produce primary products causes the production-possibility curve to shift from *AB* to *AD*. The terms of trade changes in slope from *TT* to *ZZ*. U countries now produce at *Q*, and they will still export primary products and import manufactures, but they cannot reach the point *C* because the terms of trade have worsened.

in Figure 5-4 we have a case in which U countries are *worse off* after expansion than before.[12]

In this situation, U countries argue that they should not expand their capacity to produce primary products, but should instead channel investment into manufacturing industry. They hope and believe that the new industries will be efficient and their products competitive in world markets. That is, they seek to shift the production-possibility curve from *AB* to *EB*, as in Figure 5-5. Even at the same external terms of trade (slope of *YY* = slope of

---

[12] If U countries could bargain collectively, they could restrict exports and prevent the adverse shift in the terms of trade (from *TT* to *ZZ* in Figure 5-4). The individual nation could accomplish little by restricting its own exports, however. The alert reader will observe that we have slightly altered the concept of a production possibility curve by introducing the notion that once new resources are allocated in a certain way, they are fixed and cannot be shifted.

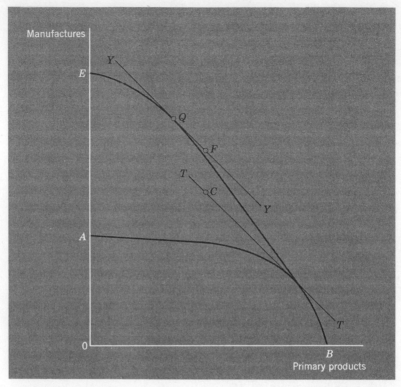

Figure 5-5. Expansion of capacity in manufacturing industry causes the production possibility to shift from *AB* to *EB*. U countries may now find it profitable to export manufactures. In this case, with terms of trade unchanged (slope of *YY* equal to *TT*), U countries may export manufactures, import primary products, and reach a point such as *F*, where they are better off than before.

TT), U countries could export manufactures and reach a higher consumption point (*F*) than they could reach before expansion. The expansion of manufacturing industries causes such a change in the structure of production that U countries develop a comparative advantage in manufactures. (The more realistic case, in which U countries continue to export some raw materials and also develop selected lines of manufacturing exports, while continuing to import complex capital goods from A countries, cannot be shown in our two-dimensional diagram.)

This view of the potential role of trade in the development of U countries clearly rests upon the belief that they can develop efficient and competitive manufacturing industries. In essence, therefore, it is a massive application of the "infant industry" argument that we examined in Chapter 3. Because the outlook for expansion of traditional exports is so gloomy, U countries believe that their best hope lies in developing manufacturing industries. They are prepared to use tariffs, quotas, subsidies, state enterprise, or any other measures that seem to promise successful development. The trouble is: no measure offers any guarantee of success. It is a fateful gamble!

III. TRADE POLICIES FOR THE FUTURE

With this view of the future of world trade, underdeveloped countries are dissatisfied with existing organizations and policies for the regulation of trade. They urge the need for new policies and new institutions to supply the special needs for underdeveloped countries.

The principal international organization through which nations negotiate and regulate commercial policies has the odd name, General Agreement on Tariffs and Trade (GATT).[13] GATT's principal function is to call international conferences at which member nations can engage in tariff bargaining on a multilateral basis. Its articles of agreement also constitute a code of behavior and a set of rules governing the conduct of trade.

In 1968, GATT had 76 members, including 20 advanced and 56 underdeveloped countries. About 40 other underdeveloped countries have declined to join GATT, and those who have joined have taken very little part in its principal activity—tariff bargaining. Underdeveloped countries have long been critical of GATT. They call it the "rich countries' club."

The main reason for this dislike is that GATT's chief purpose is to encourage nations to reduce tariffs and other trade barriers

---

[13] GATT was created in 1947, when the United States Congress sealed the fate of the more ambitious International Trade Organization by refusing to ratify its charter. The United States became a member of GATT by Executive Agreement, an uneasy solution that has existed from that day to this.

on a multilateral, reciprocal, nondiscriminatory basis. It is based on the traditional view of trade theory—the proposition that steps toward free trade are a good thing for all concerned—and on a principle of equity that calls for each nation to make concessions in exchange for those it asks of others. Underdeveloped countries argue, on the other hand, that tariff bargaining is extremely unequal when it takes place between rich, powerful nations and poor, weak ones, and that *reciprocal* free trade between advanced and underdeveloped countries will simply force U countries to remain in primary production, subject to all the disadvantages of such specialization.

U countries also argue that their developmental plans require them to limit imports to those goods that are essential for economic development. They must maintain strict controls over nonessential imports, whether by tariff, quota, or other means, in order to conserve their scarce supply of foreign exchange. They are therefore in no position to engage in the kind of negotiations that GATT sponsors.

Against these arguments it should be said that GATT's articles of agreement contain many loopholes which permit U countries to retain their import restrictions. No underdeveloped country has been hindered significantly in its control of imports by any commitment to GATT. Furthermore, U countries have benefitted from tariff reductions negotiated through GATT even when they made no concessions themselves and were not even a party to the agreements. The reason is that when a nation reduces a tariff GATT rules require that the reduction apply to imports from all nations, not just to the nation that has offered a concession in return.[14] Therefore, when advanced countries negotiate tariff reductions among themselves, the reduced rates of duty apply to exports from underdeveloped countries as well, even though the latter have made no concessions themselves. They get something for nothing. (However, U-country spokesmen would be

[14] This is what is known as the "most-favored-nation clause." The name is not very descriptive, but what it means is that when two nations agree to a mutual tariff reduction—say the United States reduces its tariff on cameras and in exchange Germany reduces its tariff on tractors—both countries agree to extend the tariff cuts on these products to imports from all other countries as well. In this way a nation's tariff rates remain uniform to all countries.

quick to point out that most of the tariff reductions made by A countries do not affect the types of goods actually exported by U countries. This may change in the future if U countries succeed in developing new lines of production.)

It was dissatisfaction with GATT, plus a generally skeptical attitude toward existing trading arrangements, that led to the United Nations Conference for Trade and Development (UNCTAD) at Genera in May 1964. Attended by 122 nations (about 90 of them underdeveloped), UNCTAD became a forum for the expression of discontent with the role of trade in development. Eighty or 90 underdeveloped nations voted again and again for resolutions and "principles," while advanced countries most often abstained or voted against the motions. Although the actions taken by UNCTAD are not binding on any nation, they nevertheless reflect the vigorous and strongly held opinions of the present governments of underdeveloped countries. UNCTAD solved no problems, but it did bring some of the issues more clearly into focus.

The dissatisfaction with GATT that was expressed at the Geneva conference soon spurred that organization to action. Before UNCTAD had even adjourned, the GATT Secretariat had drawn up the text for a new chapter in the general agreement on trade and development. All three articles in this chapter deal with the trade of underdeveloped countries, and they bear a striking similarity to the main proposals for a "new trade policy" put forward at UNCTAD. These new articles were accepted by the GATT executive board early in 1965 and then went to member governments for ratification.

As a result of resolutions adopted at the 1964 UNCTAD, the conference on Trade and Development became a permanent agency of the United Nations, and a second conference was held in 1968. At UNCTAD II, held in New Delhi, U countries again expressed their dissatisfaction with their role in world trade, and also their distress at the lack of progress since UNCTAD I.

In the following pages we shall not dwell on the respective roles of GATT and UNCTAD, but shall instead describe the main policy proposals concerning the trade of underdeveloped countries that have been put forward in recent years. These proposals fall naturally into two groups: those applying to existing trade and those applying to possible trade developments in the future. These proposals do not, by any means, command universal agreement. At the end of our discussion we shall give a brief statement of the opposing view, but our main purpose is to set forth the point of view of the underdeveloped countries.

A. *Policies for Existing Trade*

First, U countries want to expand the market for their traditional exports of food and raw materials. They urge A countries to remove their tariffs and other restrictions on such products. Although advanced countries already admit some products duty free, a great many restrictions still exist.[15] In some cases the tariff is zero but an internal consumption tax is levied. For example, internal taxes on coffee amount to 100% on import value in Germany, and 134% in Italy. Such taxes raise the price to consumers and tend to reduce consumption. In other cases, advanced countries protect domestic producers through subsidy, quota, or tariff, leaving only a residual market, if any, for imports from U countries. Agricultural protection in Europe and the United States is the principal culprit, but other products face similar barriers. The United States gives special protection to its copper, lead, and zinc producers, for example.

Such barriers to primary product exports have been widespread, but the extent to which they obstruct trade has not been fully realized until recently. One reason is that information about such barriers is more difficult to obtain and summarize than data on tariff levels. In one extreme case, Uruguay claimed that 30 products, constituting 97% of its total exports, were subject to 576 specific restrictions in 19 A countries.[16] In recent years, especially since UNCTAD, many such restrictions have been unilaterally abolished by A countries, but others are more intractable because they involve sensitive political issues.

Second, U countries want some international action taken to

[15] The interested reader will find an authoritative description of such restrictions in *World Economic Survey 1963* (New York: United Nations, 1964) Chapter 5.
[16] S. B. Linder, "The Significance of GATT for Underdeveloped Countries," Contributed Paper 6, UN Conference on Trade and Development, January 21, 1964 (mimeographed).

assure them of stabler prices and markets for their chief exports. They urge greater use of international commodity agreements, signed by the major producing and consuming countries, to stabilize prices at "remunerative" levels. Nearly everyone agrees that reduction of price fluctuation would be desirable, but this simple-sounding objective has proved extraordinarily difficult to accomplish in practice. Vast amounts of thought, energy, and time have gone into international commodity agreements, but the record is an unbroken one of almost total failure.

One reason for the poor record is that participating nations disagree about the major objective of an agreement or about the best way to achieve it. The objectives of commodity stabilization may be (1) to reduce the range of price fluctuations around the long-term trend, (2) to *raise* the price above its long-term trend, (3) to stabilize export proceeds instead of price, or (4) to stabilize income of individual producers in the exporting countries. These objectives are sometimes in conflict with one another, and U countries are not always clear or consistent about their priorities among them.

Other difficulties are both practical and technical. When a buffer stock is used, storage costs may be heavy. Commodities must, of course, be physically capable of storage without deterioration, a condition that rules out the use of buffer stocks in many cases. Financial resources must also be available to enable the buffer stock to buy and hold a sizable quantity of the commodity. When the price is being supported, whether by buffer stock purchases or reduced production in participating countries, there is a danger that other countries will increase their output and benefit from their nonparticipation. In the 1930s, for example, Thailand at first declined to join the international rubber agreement and Thai exports sharply increased at favorable prices when the participating countries reduced *their* exports in order to increase the price of rubber.[17] Many countries have learned, to their sorrow, that substitution effects can be powerful and difficult to circumvent. Action by a group of countries to increase the price of a product may encourage the growth of competing producers of that same product (as in the case of rubber, just men-

[17] Thailand later joined the agreement with a very favorable export quota.

tioned, or coffee, when Brazilian export restrictions encouraged the development of African coffee-growing), or it may encourage the development of substitutes. The market system has a vitality and resiliency that must be kept clearly in mind when schemes to manipulate it are being drawn up.

One of the gravest practical problems is also the most obvious: selection of the price targets. If the lower support—the "floor price"—is set too high, unwieldy stocks accumulate or production quotas have to be steadily cut; if the upper limit—the "ceiling price"—is set too low, the buffer stock may quickly be exhausted. If an attempt is made to keep price higher than its long-run trend level, severe export curbs are necessary in member countries, and outsiders have a strong inducement to expand their output. In their choice of price targets, the framers of international commodity agreements have all too often been poor prophets!

Some of these problems can be illustrated by a brief description of two existing agreements for tin and coffee. The International Tin Agreement provides for a buffer stock, with variable export quotas for member countries to be used to adapt supply to changes in demand. The Tin Council sets upper and lower price limits; within that price range the buffer-stock manager has discretion over buffer-stock transactions. Operation began in 1956 under the present agreement (several other tin control schemes had preceded this one). The buffer-stock manager had £16 million, equal to 25,000 tons of tin at the floor price. For the first few months the price of tin hovered at the lower support level, but it dropped during the 1958 recession and purchases of tin soon exhausted the funds available. The price of tin fell through the floor for a brief period in 1958. In the meantime, producer members had accepted sharp reductions in their export quotas, and they had, in turn, cut back the production of tin at the mines. When the demand for tin began to rise, producer members were reluctant to raise export quotas because of fear of spoiling the market, and the buffer-stock manager was soon selling tin at the ceiling price. The buffer stock was exhausted in 1961, and the price of tin went through the ceiling. Export quotas were subsequently removed, but a strong demand for tin kept the price high. The Tin Council raised the price ceiling from $1.10 to $1.75 in a series of steps, but even so the market price remained above the ceiling specified by the Tin Council until the last increase in the ceiling in 1966. Because it had no tin, the buffer had no influence on price. After 1966 the market price declined, and in 1968 it began to approach the floor price. The buffer-stock manager again bought tin to support its price, and export quotas were reduced. Figure 5-6 shows the behavior of the tin price and its relation to the floor and ceiling prices of the Tin Council.

Whether the tin agreement has reduced instability in tin prices and export proceeds is an open question. Other important factors influencing the market were the United States stockpile, sales from which have helped to restrain the rise in price, sales of tin by Soviet Russia, and the sharp decline in Indonesian exports.

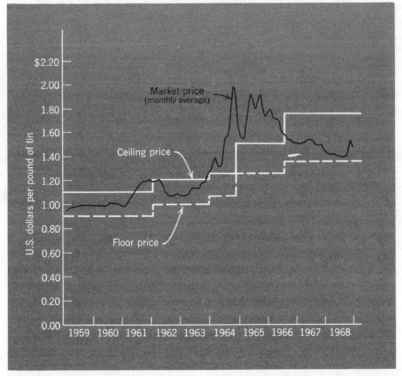

Figure 5-6. Tin prices, 1959–1968. Floor and ceiling prices set in the International Tin Agreement have been progressively increased since 1956. *Source. International Financial Statistics,* International Monetary Fund.

That troubled country, once the second largest tin exporter, sold only 12,000 tons in 1966.

The most recent of many efforts to stabilize the price of coffee culminated in the International Coffee Agreement of 1962. Under this agreement coffee-exporting countries agreed to limit their exports to quotas assigned by the International Coffee Council. Importing countries agreed to limit imports from nonmember countries to a fixed level, thus giving member countries the benefit of any increase in world coffee consumption. This provision also provided an incentive for producing countries to become members, and reduced the likelihood that the agreement would be undermined by an expansion of nonmember production. Importing countries also agreed to require a certificate of origin for all coffee imports and to keep a record of the amount imported from each country. Importing countries therefore perform an essential function in policing the agreement; without this check on imports there would be no way to enforce the export quotas and, particularly, to limit imports from nonmembers.

The agreement provided for no central buffer stock, but each producing country is responsible for controlling production and managing the stock of coffee within its borders. The real control over supply rests on the export quotas set for member countries. By adjusting these, supply can be adjusted to demand.

The 1962 agreement was vague about price targets. No upper and lower limits were specified, but one clear objective was to prevent any further *decline* in the price of coffee. The price of coffee had fallen rather steadily from its peak in 1953 to 1962 (see Figure 5-1). Producing countries wanted to stop this decline in price, and they could agree on a floor price, but they were reluctant to set a rigid ceiling price. This vagueness about price targets was a major stumbling block in persuading importing countries to join. In particular, the United States Congress feared that the agreement would be used to force up the price of coffee, thus exploiting the United States consumer. The United States alone buys about one half of all coffee exports.

Experience to date has been mixed. Coffee prices rose sharply in 1963 when the Brazilian crop, one half of the world's output, was cut 50% by bad weather. Since that time, the price has slowly drifted downward, but it has remained above the low level reached in 1962 (see Figure 5-1).

This degree of success in stabilizing coffee prices has been achieved largely through export quotas and production controls. When production exceeded export quotas, producing countries undertook to keep the surplus off the market, and to reduce it by cutting back production. Nevertheless, the surplus overhanging the market rose steadily from 1957 to 1966, by which date it was equal to about 14 months' consumption. The surplus declined slightly from 1966 to 1968—a hopeful sign for price stability.

The International Coffee Agreement was revised in 1968 and extended for another five years. At that time, 66 producer and consumer nations, accounting for almost all of the world's coffee trade, were participating in the agreement. The new agreement is similar to the original one in most important respects, but it does provide some inducement to producer countries to diversify their agricultural sectors and thus reduce coffee production.

Although the renewal of this agreement reflects a degree of success, problems do lie ahead. For one thing, growth in consumption of coffee has slowed, partly because of high tariffs and internal taxes in consuming countries, and partly because of the popularity of other beverages which are substitutes for coffee.

Despite the poor record of international commodity agreements, many people think they have promise. Prebisch says "there can be no doubt that the obstacle here is primarily political rather than technical," echoing Gunnar Myrdal a decade earlier, who argued that failure occurred because of the lack of "human solidarity between nations."[18] Prebisch also makes it clear that he wants to raise, and not merely stabilize, the prices of U-country exports. This objective makes the task of formulating workable commodity agreements doubly difficult, and the burden of proof seems to fall on Prebisch and others to show how to do it.

Third, U countries want to be protected against adverse movements in their terms of trade. If their terms of trade continue to deteriorate, with or without commodity agreements, U countries

[18] *Towards a New Trade Policy for Development,* op. cit., p. 57; G. Myrdal, *The International Economy* (New York: Harper, 1956), p. 250.

want to be compensated so that their ability to import will be unimpaired. Such compensation would enable development plans to be carried on without interruption.

The potential loss in real imports through adverse terms of trade is very large. For example, if U-country exports are $25 billion, a 10% fall in their terms of trade means a loss of $2.5 billion of imports, an amount about equal to United States foreign aid (in the form of grants) in recent years.

Most official studies and discussions of compensation schemes have thus far been concerned with short-term *lending* to cushion the impact on a country of a sharp fall in its export proceeds. U countries would prefer some kind of insurance scheme to provide outright compensation to a country whose export proceeds had declined. They want A countries to join them in making contributions (premium payments) to the insurance fund. Several such schemes have been proposed, but none of them has won wide support. A countries are reluctant to commit themselves to provide economic aid on an automatic basis, such as these schemes imply.

Fourth, U countries fear that customs unions among A countries will have an adverse effect on their trade. Specifically, they fear that the European Common Market will keep its external tariff high, thus encouraging the growth of trade within the Common Market at the expense of imports from the outside world. We shall examine this matter in more detail in the next chapter. U countries want to prevent the discriminatory effect of customs unions. This policy objective applies to both existing exports and potential new ones.

B. *Policies to Encourage New Exports*

First, U countries want A countries to reduce their tariffs on new export products, particularly exports of manufactures. By reducing or eliminating tariffs on such goods, A countries will provide a market large enough to permit new industries in U countries to produce at the most efficient scale. It is often argued that they are handicapped because they cannot build plants large enough to obtain the full economies of large-scale production.

U countries are particularly anxious to eliminate tariffs that discriminate against processed materials. Many A countries have

low (or zero) tariffs on unprocessed materials, but charge higher
and higher tariffs as the stage of processing advances. Table 5-5
contains a few specific examples of these differential tariffs. In
such cases, the "effective tariff," or duty collected as a percentage
of value-added in manufacture, is higher than the "nominal tariff"
on goods in the more advanced stages of processing or manufacture. The economic effect is to encourage the import of the unprocessed material and to discourage the development of simple
processing industries in the U countries concerned. The discriminatory effect can be extremely powerful. For example, if 100 lb
of jute yarn is valued at $60 in the world market, while 100 lb of
raw jute is worth $50, the value-added in manufacture is $10, or
20%. If a 12% tariff is charged on jute yarn, while raw jute is
admitted free of tariff, the "effective tariff" to the spinning industry is 72%. That is, the tariff on yarn imports as a percentage
of *value-added* in spinning would be 72%.[19]

Recent discussion of the "effective tariff" concept has dramatized the fact that the existing tariff structure hampers U
countries in their efforts to follow the dictates of comparative
advantage and develop industries to process the primary products they export. For their part, A countries resist any significant
expansion in their imports of processed materials if such imports
pose any threat to domestic producers.

The United States response to imports of Brazilian instant
coffee illustrates this problem. Brazil, the world's largest coffee
exporter, recently began to install plants to produce instant coffee.
These plants were able to compete with U.S. producers because
they could buy broken beans at prices well below the world price
for regular coffee beans, because they saved transport cost (two
thirds of weight is lost in the manufacturing process), and because they could pay lower wage rates. Before long, Brazilian
producers had captured some 14% of the United States' instant
coffee market, and U.S. producers were demanding relief. After
negotiations between the two governments, Brazil agreed to impose an *export* tax on instant coffee large enough to offset the

[19] A 12% duty on yarn imports with $60 would be $7.20. The ratio of this
duty to value-added is 72% ($7.20 ÷ $10). See Bela Balassa, *Trade Liberalization Among Industrial Countries* (New York: McGraw Hill, 1967),
Ch. 3.

Table 5-5. Tariff Rates in United States and Europe, by Commodity and Stage of Processing (Percentage)

Commodity	Tariff Rates (Percentages)		
	E.E.C.[a]	United Kingdom	United States
Cotton			
Raw	0	0	0
Yarn	8	8	14
Jute			
Raw	0	0	0
Yarn	10	13	20
Cocoa			
Beans	9	1½	0
Powder	27	13	4
Iron and Steel			
Ore	0	0	0
Pig iron	7	4	9
Finished articles	9	14	10
Leather			
Hides and skins	0	0	0
Leather, finished	7	13	10
Leather footwear	16	15	13

Source. World Economic Survey, 1962 (New York: U.N., 1963) p. 79; *World Economic Survey,* 1963 (New York: U.N., 1964) p. 186.
[a] E.E.C. stands for the European Economic Community. The tariff rates given here represent the common external tariff rates for the six member nations.

advantage her producers enjoy through the low prices they pay for broken beans. This agreement, forced upon Brazil by the United States, denies the principle of comparative advantage and prevents the development of a resource-based manufacturing industry that seems obvious and natural for Brazil. Such episodes do not increase the confidence that U countries have for the economic principles espoused by A countries.

U countries do not want to match the tariff reductions asked of A countries. Reciprocity is abandoned. U countries argue that they must control the composition of their imports in order to carry out their development plans, that they will, in any case, buy as many imports as their export earnings will allow, and that the GATT concept of reciprocity in tariff bargaining should not apply to bargains between advanced and underdeveloped countries.

Second, U countries go even further and ask A countries to give them tariff *preferences.* That is, they want the tariff reductions made by A countries to apply only to imports from U countries. They want to abandon the GATT principle of nondiscrimination and the "most-favored-nation clause."[20] Such tariff preferences might be temporary, for instance, for a 10-year-period, and they might apply only to a fixed dollar amount of imports in each category. For example, the United States might be asked to lower its tariff on bicycles imported from U countries by 30% to 5%, the reduced duty to apply to $50,000,000 of imports. Imports of bicycles from A countries would continue to pay the full tariff of 30%. Such an action would create a preferential market of $50,000,000 for new exports from U countries, and would encourage their producers to expand production. The hope is that expanded production would bring a reduction in cost per bicycle. This argument stems from the infant-industry argument, and rests upon the belief that economies of scale are important. The argument is that when plant size increases, the minimum point on the average total curve declines. For example, in Figure 5-7 the minimum average cost for a small-scale bicycle plant is $75 for an output of 1000 bicycles, but when plant size is increased (ATC_2) the minimum average cost drops to $40 for an output of 5000 bicycles.

Tariff protection in the U country itself may not be enough to enable producers to achieve an efficient scale of production because the domestic market is so small. In that case, infant-industry protection will fail to achieve its purpose. The appeal for preferential treatment in A-country markets is an ingenious attempt to overcome this deficiency.

At the first session of the United Nations Conference on Trade Development (UNCTAD I), U countries urged A countries to grant them such preferences on their exports of manufactures, but they did not make much headway. Many A countries, including the United States, were opposed in principle to preferential tariffs. At the second session (UNCTAD II), in 1968, this was

[20] See footnote 14.

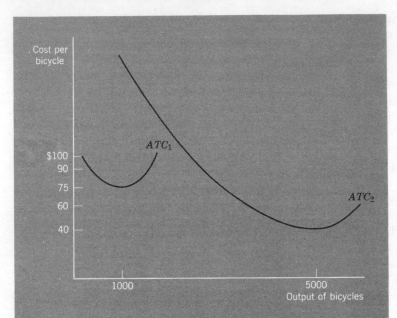

Figure 5-7. Average cost per bicycle in small and large plants.

the paramount issue. This time, it was unanimously agreed that such preferences should be established at an early date. Despite this agreement on the principle, little progress has been made in working out the details of specific arrangements to extend preferences.

Third, U countries call for preferential tariff arrangements among the underdeveloped countries themselves. U countries could reduce tariffs on imports from one another, perhaps by creating customs unions or free-trade areas among groups of underdeveloped countries. Such regional groupings would increase the size of the market available to the producer. Steps have been taken in Central America and in Latin America to form regional trade associations but, thus far, their success has been limited.

Access to markets in advanced countries is the crucial issue in expanding exports of U countries. Much depends upon the willingness of A countries to accept a rising volume of imports, especially imports of manufactured goods. As yet the volume of manufactured imports from U countries is too small to give us much indication of what to expect. However, we can mention one favorable and one unfavorable factor. The favorable factor is that an enormous increase in trade in manufactures has taken place among A countries in recent years. It rose from $25 billion to $79 billion between 1958 and 1967. If A countries are willing to exchange manufactured goods among themselves, why should they object to trade with U countries, exchanging complex manufactures for simple ones? Furthermore, a substantial reduction in tariff rates has occurred in A countries, and these reductions also apply to imports from U countries because of the most-favored-nation clause. If U countries can produce manufactured goods at competitive prices, they will not face inordinately high tariff walls when they begin to export these goods.

The unfavorable factor is that a hostile reception has met the one item of manufactured goods that U countries have begun to export in sizable volume—textiles. When American and European imports began to rise sharply, their domestic textile producers sought protection. For a time the exporting nations voluntarily restricted their exports in an effort to prevent drastic curbs from being applied by importing nations, and finally an International Cotton Textile Agreement was negotiated in 1962. This Agreement sets quotas for cotton textile imports into the major importing nation. The quotas are supposed to increase over the term of the agreement, thus allowing an orderly growth in imports. One of the main objectives is to avoid "market disruption" in the principal importing countries.

The effect of the textile agreement is to set definite limits on the access of U countries to A-country markets for textiles. Many observers believe that a similar reluctance to admit manufacturing imports will appear whenever U countries become competitive in a new line of production, and they therefore conclude that the prospects for a major expansion of U-country exports are dim indeed. However, this may be too gloomy a view. The textile industry *is* a special case. In the United States the issue of agricultural support and "two-price cotton" was involved, and in both Europe and the United States important political issues were present. Textile plants are concentrated in particular regions, often those that are already suffering from low income and high rates of unemployment. It is possible that other manufactured imports will find a less hostile reception than textiles. The entire world will be watching to see what happens, since no other factor is so vital in determining the future course of trade and development.

IV. A BRIEF REBUTTAL: THE OLD ORTHODOXY

We have presented the U-countries' point of view, and emphasized their case for skepticism about the role of trade in economic development. To state that case forcefully, we have deliberately refrained from counterarguments except in certain places. The U-countries' point of view is important, influential, and extremely widespread; the informed citizen should be aware of it. He should also be aware of its limitations, however, and we shall therefore comment briefly on the opposing view.[21]

The "new orthodoxy" of the U countries is challenged at almost every point by some economists. The factual proof of an adverse trend in U-country terms of trade is disputed, as we mentioned in a previous section. Predictions of an adverse trend in the future terms of trade are disputed just as vigorously. Indeed, some economists believe that the pressure of population on resources may, at last, confirm the classical expectation and cause the terms of trade to move strongly in favor of food and raw materials. According to this view, an underdeveloped country would be wise to expand its capacity to produce primary products and thus be in a position to reap the gains from trade.

Many economists dispute the reasons given for the lagging exports of U countries.[22] They say that exports lag, not because of sagging export markets, but because of unwise policies in exporting countries. When money demand is stimulated and imports of consumer goods are sharply restricted, domestic resources are diverted into domestic substitutes and away from export indus-

---

[21] For a fuller analysis and evaluation of the trade grumbles of U countries, see G. M. Meier, *International Economics of Development* (New York: Harper & Row, 1968), Chapters 7-9.

[22] Incidentally, the lag in exports is much less pronounced if petroleum is included. Consequently, advocates of the "new orthodoxy" omit petroleum, opponents include it.

tries. Overvaluation of currencies has the same effect. Governments in U countries often deny export industries the right to buy imported machinery to improve productivity, and they impose heavy taxes on exports. The expected result is a decline in exports. When governments discourage trade and place obstacles in its way, they should not claim that the declining role of trade is proof that the market economy no longer works properly!

Nearly everyone accepts the *logic* of the case for infant-industry protection,[23] but the dissenters believe it has only limited practical usefulness. They emphasize the difficulties of selecting the right industries to protect. When infant industries fail to grow up, the cost of permanent protection can be extremely heavy.

Dissenters also believe that competitive pressures from the world market perform a valuable function in keeping producers on their toes. Nothing is more conducive to laziness and inefficiency than a sheltered market! The test of competition is still the best stimulus to efficiency known to man, and U countries are advised to make much use of it.

On one point there is agreement—barriers to trade in A countries should be removed. The whole apparatus of internal fiscal charges to hold down consumption, of discriminatory tariff rates on processed raw materials, and of quotas to protect domestic producers is now under attack. To remove it will be a long, painful task, but few economists will attempt to defend it, logically.

Much of the grumbling about unfair division of the gains from trade can be dismissed as "the economics of self-pity." U countries have certainly sought a scapegoat on which to blame their failure to achieve a satisfactory rate of economic growth. But the suspicion remains that there is more to it than that. We cannot resolve this debate, since it is, after all, one of the great issues of our time.

[23] At the United Nations Conference on Trade and Development, Special Principle Four ("developing countries have the right to protect their infant industries") was adopted by a vote of 115 to none, with one abstention. The abstainer: the United States.

6

European Economic Integration and World Trade

When a shipment of merchandise moves by truck or train from Boston to Atlanta, or from Chicago to Los Angeles, it need stop only for traffic signals, or perhaps for a check of weight limits. Otherwise, no barriers exist to hinder the movement of goods. Until recently, when a similar shipment moved from Amsterdam to Rome, or from Paris to Copenhagen, it had to stop for inspection and clearance every time it crossed a national frontier. The journey required masses of permits, stamps, and other documentation, with an import tariff to be paid in the country of final destination. In contrast to the large, open, *common market* in the United States, the economy of Western Europe was, until recently, fragmented into many separate nations, each jealous of its sovereignty and anxious to safeguard "domestic" interests against "foreign" competition.

This sharp contrast between the integrated economy of the United States of America and the compartmentalized economy of Europe has been emphasized for a century or more, and European statesmen and thinkers have often proposed the creation of a United States of Europe. No serious prospect of this development appeared until the 1950s, however, after Europe had survived two world wars and seen its political and economic power eclipsed by the rise of the United States and the U.S.S.R.

During the stress of postwar reconstruction and under the tension of the Soviet threat, Western Europe took the first hesitant steps toward economic integration.

At first, the hope was that all of Western Europe could be included in a single integrated market. In the administration of economic aid under the Marshall Plan, the United States constantly urged European nations toward economic cooperation. At United States' insistence, the Organization for European Economic Cooperation (OEEC) was created to allocate aid funds. It soon began to handle other important economic functions as well and, for a time, it appeared that the OEEC might evolve into an economic union to include all 17 member nations. The dream of a fully united Europe failed to materialize, however, and only 6 nations finally signed the Treaty of Rome in 1957 to create the European Economic Community. The Rome treaty is nevertheless an important turning point in European history, since it creates a far-reaching economic union between those ancient enemies, France and Germany, and Italy, Belgium, Luxembourg, and the Netherlands. Thus it creates a geographically compact economic entity with a population of 186 million and a gross national product of $322 billion (1966), second only to the United States.

I. CENTRAL PROVISIONS OF THE TREATY OF ROME

The Treaty of Rome is primarily an economic document. The economic union that it creates has profound political implications, but these are not made explicit; they are left to be worked out in the future. The conferees were wise enough to see that no consensus on political matters had yet evolved. Many urgent political questions still remain unsettled, and the European Economic Community may face its gravest tests when these questions must finally be grappled with. Our emphasis throughout this chapter is upon the economic aspects of the European Economic Community (EEC) and its effects upon Europe and the rest of the world.

The clear objective of the Rome treaty is to create an economic union within which trade and other economic transactions will be as free as they are within the United States. To achieve this objective, the member countries have agreed to the following key provisions:

1. To remove tariffs, quotas, and other barriers to trade within the community.
2. To adopt a uniform external tariff on goods coming in from the outside world.
3. To allow free movement of labor, capital, and enterprise within the community.
4. To establish a common agricultural policy, a common transport policy, and a common policy toward competition and business practices.
5. To harmonize and coordinate monetary and fiscal policies, social policies, and even to equalize wages for men and women.

Other provisions establish a European Investment Bank, a social fund, and a set of governing institutions including a council, a commission, an assembly, and a court of justice. Provision is also made for overseas territories of the six member countries to be associated with the EEC, and for other nations to become associates or even full members of the EEC. Admission to full membership requires a unanimous vote of member countries. This last provision is of particular interest in view of Britain's abortive attempt to join.

The Rome treaty wisely provided for a transitional period of 12 to 15 years during which the objectives were to be attained. The time schedule is flexible, and can be lengthened or shortened as desired. However, the EEC should be in full operation by 1972, 15 years after the Treaty of Rome.

The most dramatic and perhaps the most important feature of the EEC has been its creation of a customs union. To achieve such a union, two steps are required: internal barriers must be eliminated, and a common external tariff must be decided upon. A time table was specified for both of these steps. Internal tariffs on industrial goods were to be abolished by a series of 10 separate 10% reductions, spread over the transition period. (Agriculture receives special treatment.) Under the original time table, internal tariffs would have reached zero in December, 1969, but the six member nations accelerated the pace and abolished in-

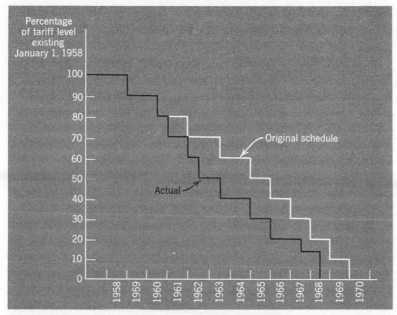

Figure 6-1. Original schedule and actual progress on removal of internal tariffs on industrial goods. These tariffs are those levied by EEC members on imports from one another. Such tariffs reached zero, effective July 1, 1968.

ternal tariffs July 1, 1968. Figure 6-1 compares actual tariff cut: with those originally planned.

For most products the common external tariff is fixed at the arithmetic average of tariff rates prevailing in member nations in 1957. In this calculation the Benelux countries are treated as a single unit, so the average of four tariff rates becomes the common external tariff.[1] For example, if preunion duties on product X were:

Benelux	8%
Germany	14
France	30
Italy	40

[1] The EEC reduced its common external tariff 20% across the board in 1962. This reduction was made in connection with GATT negotiations for reciprocal tariff cuts between the EEC and other nations. Benelux is an economic union that predated the EEC; its members are Belgium, Netherlands, and Luxembourg.

the common external tariff would be 23% [(8 + 14 + 30 + 40) ÷ 4 = 23]. The EEC adopted this formula because of a GATT requirement that a customs union should not increase the average level of tariffs existing in member nations prior to formation of the union.

Prior to union, tariff rates in Germany and the Benelux countries were generally lower than those of France and Italy. Therefore, adjustment to the common level required an increase in German and Benelux rates, and a decrease in French and Italian rates. Outside countries whose exports go mainly to Germany will find the average level of tariffs *higher* than the preunion level. Figure 6-2 contains a schematic diagram to illustrate the typical pattern of national adjustments. Adjustment of national tariffs to the common external tariff level took place in three steps:

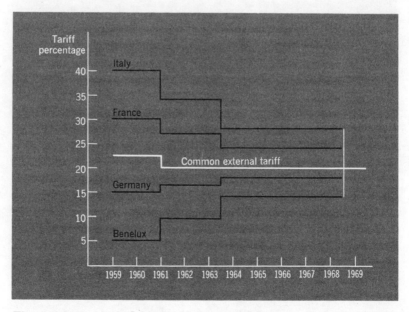

Figure 6-2. Time schedule for adjustment of national tariffs to the common external level for a hypothetical product. In the adjustment to a common level, in most cases German and Benelux tariff rates must be increased, while French and Italian rates must be reduced. *Source.* Chase Manhattan Bank, *The European Common Market.*

30% in 1961, 30% in 1963, and 40% on July 1, 1968. Thus the common external tariff became effective simultaneously with the abolition of the last internal tariffs within the EEC.

Besides agriculture, a number of articles were exempted from the arithmetic average formula. The common tariff levels for these articles were settled by negotiation among the six member nations. Although outside countries feared that protectionist sentiment would be strong in these cases, the rates finally set were not much higher than those that would have resulted from the formula—with a few notable exceptions.

The EEC is more than a customs union; it is also a *common market*. Elimination of all internal tariffs and other restrictions creates one large market area within which producers are free to compete for the consumer's franc, mark, or lira. But even more is provided: labor and capital are free to move about within the Community, and an entrepreneur can set up his factory or store wherever he wishes. No doubt the ties of family, language, and culture will prevent labor and capital from being perfectly mobile, but at least the legal barriers to movement will be removed.

The authors of the Rome treaty wisely foresaw that when the six member nations became one large common market, a great many social and economic policies would have to be coordinated —policies that had formerly been the separate concern of each individual nation. The need to harmonize some policies is fairly obvious, as in the case of setting railway rates. The objective of the common market would be thwarted if France, for example, set railway rates very low and thus enabled French producers to undersell Italian producers in the German market. Hence, a common transport policy became necessary.

Other cases are much less obvious, such as the need to harmonize social-security schemes because, otherwise, firms might obtain a competitive advantage by moving to the country with the lowest benefits (hence lowest taxes), or the need to have a common policy on antitrust and monopoly problems because, otherwise, firms in one country could have an unfair advantage. Indeed, in the areas of monetary and fiscal policy, the extent to which coordination and harmonization would be required was simply unknown, and member nations had to learn from experience.

Thus far, experience suggests that formation of a common market has deep and far-reaching effects on the economies of member nations, and that it requires coordination and harmonization over a wide range of policies, penetrating deeply into the national life. Much that was formerly determined independently by an autonomous nation state must now be jointly determined for the Community as a whole. Dawning recognition of the imperative requirement for community-wide action over such a range of social and economic policies has pushed political issues to the fore.

In such a full economic union as the six member nations have undertaken, one prime objective is to make the conditions of competition—the rules of the game—the same in all parts of the Community so that the fundamental "natural" advantages of resource endowment, efficiency of labor, and skill of management can be reflected in price, with the lowest-cost producers surviving in each industry. What is now being recognized perhaps should have been apparent from the start—that to make the "conditions of competition" the same requires a thoroughgoing overhaul of separate national policies to achieve uniformity. If one nation levies higher taxes than another on a particular industry, it produces a bias; or if one nation subsidizes electric power, its producers have an "unfair" advantage in the production of goods requiring much electricity.

Competition and free movements of factors also place limits on national action. For example, if a nation tries to reduce its rates of interest below the levels in other member nations, the freedom of capital movements will permit funds to flow out of the low-interest country and probably force it to abandon the attempt to reduce its rates. Similiarly, limits may be placed on wage-rate changes. If a French labor union presses for higher wages, plants may close and move to a country where wages are lower.

The scope of independent national policy is greatly narrowed; the role of the central institutions is enlarged. How much national autonomy is compatible with the emerging European Economic Community has not yet been determined.

II. ECONOMIC EFFECTS ON EUROPE

The positive case for economic integration has always been that members would derive important benefits from it. The precise nature of those benefits is often unclear; the bigger market is simply supposed to be a good thing. One job of the economist is to clarify such vague ideas. We shall mention three possible sources of benefits to member countries from an economic union.

The first is a straightforward application of the theory of trade—the argument that nations benefit from specialization and exchange. This argument was given in Chapter 2 and need not be repeated here. The chief point is that if trade among member nations is hampered by tariffs and other restrictions, elimination of these barriers will allow production to take place in the most efficient location. Each member nation can specialize in those lines of production in which it has a comparative advantage, exchanging these products for the specialities of other members. By utilizing the most efficient producers, a greater output can be obtained with given resources of land, labor, and capital. Several economists attempted empirical estimates of this portion of the gain from economic integration. In all cases the potential gain was found to be very small—around 1% of national income.

When trade barriers fall, trade among member nations expands. This is the "trade creation effect" of a common market.[2] The greater the increase in trade among member countries, the greater is the benefit from a customs union. Large benefits from increased trade also imply that much shifting of resources has occurred, with each nation expanding those industries in which it has a comparative advantage and contracting other industries.

Even though the EEC appears to be a movement toward free trade (a movement usually approved by economists), economists are by no means certain that the net benefits are positive for the world as a whole. Doubt arises because the EEC has reduced tariffs among member countries but retained a tariff wall against outside nations.[3] Thus, a degree of discrimination is introduced.

---

[2] The term was introduced by Jacob Viner, *The Customs Union Issue* (New York, Carnegie Endowment, 1950).

[3] In short, the "most-favored-nation" clause does not apply to the tariff re-

It is possible that the increase in trade among member countries is *not* newly created trade but simply a diversion of trade from the outside world.

This point can be made clear by an example. Suppose that, prior to union, France and Germany have tariffs of 60% and 40% on transistor radios, and suppose the costs of production in France, Germany, and Japan (a nonmember country) for a radio of given quality are as follows:

France	$30
Germany	$20
Japan	$15

Prior to union, France would import transistor radios from Japan, since the import price including tariff would be $24 [$15 + 60% ($15)], while Germany would produce her own [home cost, $20, is less than the import price, $21 ($15 + 40% of $15)]. When France and Germany form a customs union, however, German radios enter France free of duty and can undersell the Japanese product. In this example, if the common external tariff is set at 50% (the arithmetic average), Japanese radios would cost $22.50 in France compared to $20 for German ones. Trade between France and Japan is displaced by trade between France and Germany. Trade within the common market thus increases, but is diverted from the outside world. It is not newly created trade. The economist dislikes this outcome because it shifts production from the lowest-cost producer (Japan) to a higher-cost producer (Germany). This result is contrary to the usual free-trade effect, and it arises because the members of the customs union have discriminatory tariff rates—zero for members but a common tariff to outsiders.

The second source of benefits from economic union is our old friend: the economies of scale. Just as underdeveloped countries argue that their home markets are too small to enable their producers to build plants large enough for greatest efficiency, so European countries argue that their national markets

ductions granted to each other by EEC members. This exception was authorized by GATT under the terms of its Article 24, which permits formation of customs unions.

are too small to support firms as large as their giant competitors in the United States. This argument has made a deep impression on the popular mind. The man on the street is impressed by the fact that in many industries a single firm in the United States has a larger sales volume than the entire industry in France, Germany, or Italy.

According to *Fortune's* directory of the largest industrial firms, 175 United States firms had sales of over $500 million in 1967, compared to only 45 firms in the entire EEC. (Of these 45, 15 were French, 18 German, 7 Italian, and 5 in the Benelux countries.) Aside from multinational firms like Royal Dutch Shell, the largest industrial firm in the EEC is Volkswagen, the German automobile firm, but it would rank only 31st on the United States list. In individual industries, General Motors dwarfs its nearest European rival, Volkswagen, by $20.0 billion to $2.3 billion in total sales; International Business Machines dwarfs Olivetti ($5.3 billion to $0.5 billion); and General Electric's sales exceeded Siemens' by $7.7 billion to $2.0 billion. Although bigness does not necessarily mean efficiency and low-cost production, the two are commonly believed to be closely related.

The argument is that (1) the bigger the firm and the larger its volume of production, the lower is the cost per unit, and (2) the larger the domestic market, the larger is the number of big firms that it can support. The striking difference between the United States and European markets is then emphasized. Table 6-1 contains figures for gross national product in 1957, 1963, and 1966. The United States GNP is more than six times as large as Germany's, the largest in Europe. But the combined GNP of the six EEC nations is two-fifths the size of that of the United States. Creation of the common market thus permits European firms to expand their scale of output in a sheltered market and to achieve the economies of large-scale production, if these exist.

Economists disagree about the importance of the economies of scale. Some economists believe that in most industries the least-cost output is reached at a relatively small scale, and that further increases in the size of the firm do not bring lower costs per unit. They argue that with a GNP of $50 billion, a nation's market is big enough in most industries to enable its firms to produce at an efficient scale of output. Others believe that in

Table 6-1. Gross National Product (Billions of Dollars at Current Prices)

	1957	1963	1966
Belgium–Luxemburg	$ 10	$ 15	$ 18
Netherlands	9	15	21
France	56	81	102
Germany	51	95	120
Italy	27	49	61
Total E.E.C.	$153	$255	$322
United States	$448	$600	$756

Source. *National Accounts of OECD Countries, 1957–66,* Organization for Economic Cooperation and Development.

many manufacturing industries, the cost per unit continues to fall as the scale of output increases, up to a very large scale. Although this is a factual argument, the facts are not available to settle it conclusively. The relationship probably varies from one industry to another, and may also vary between countries. In some European countries, it is clear that total national output of certain products was not sufficient to keep several optimum-scale plants busy. For example, a rayon-yarn plant requires an output of 20,000 to 25,000 tons per year for optimal operations, but total production was only 10,000 tons in Belgium and 30,000 in the Netherlands.[4] In such cases, if tariff protection is high enough to keep the domestic industry going, costs per unit will be high. The benefits of a customs union, which will force the small, inefficient firms out of business, will therefore be great.

This discussion of the economies of scale has been limited to *internal* economies of the firm or industry. We should mention that many economists believe *external* economies may be even more important in reducing costs per unit as market size expands. However, a full discussion of this complex matter is not within the scope of this book.

The third source of benefits arises from the stimulus to competition provided by the common market. Firms that have grown fat and lazy in sheltered national markets are suddenly exposed to competition from rivals in all the other member nations. The hot winds of competition are a powerful stimulus to

---

[4] Bela Balassa, *The Theory of Economic Integration* (Homewood: Richard D. Irwin, 1961), p. 133.

managerial efficiency. Firms become acutely cost-conscious and much more receptive to technological improvements than before. The efficient, low-cost firm sees its profits rise, and investment in additional capacity is encouraged. Such new investment naturally embodies the latest technological advances, and the high rate of investment in the EEC since 1958 has therefore brought a substantial modernization of its industrial plant. This is one reason for the strong competitive position of the EEC in world trade, especially in comparison to England, where a large proportion of industrial capacity is pre-World War II vintage.

The economic effects of the common market on *member* nations are basically the same as the effects of free trade, presented in Chapter 2. Member nations are, after all, accepting completely free trade among themselves. These effects are: (1) a shift, or reallocation, of resources in each country into those industries in which it possesses a comparative advantage and out of other industries; (2) an equalization of commodity prices throughout the community, except for differences owing to transport costs; (3) a tendency toward equalization of wage rates, reinforced in this case by the provision that workers can move freely from one country to another; and (4) a tendency toward equalization of interest rates. These four effects result in (5) an increase in economic welfare (real income) as resources are utilized more efficiently.

It seems likely that, as firms grow larger and begin to produce for a Community-wide market, products will become standardized and advertising will be employed to develop a mass market. Many Europeans fear that the requirements of mass production and marketing will inexorably force society itself to become standardized and homogenized. They fear the loss of diversity and certain distinctive aspects of national life. Such a loss would offset some of the economic benefits of integration.

The founding fathers of the EEC have good reason to be pleased with its performance thus far. Member nations have enjoyed high rates of growth in income, full employment, strong balances of payments, rapidly expanding trade, and a high level of investment. How much of this good fortune is due to the common market cannot be determined, but most observers think that the connection is close. GNP in the Community as a whole rose 110% (at current prices) from 1957 to 1966. After adjusting for price increases, the annual rate of growth in real output was about 5.5%. Unemployment has been near zero throughout this period. However, EEC nations were growing rapidly even before 1958, and the causal connection between formation of the common market and high growth rates has not been proved.

Trade of EEC nations has expanded greatly since 1957. Trade within the EEC rose from $7.9 billion in 1957 to $24.5 billion in 1967, an increase of 210%. Exports from the rest of the world to the EEC also rose from $16.2 billion to $28.1 billion in the same period, an increase of 74%. Table 6-2 contains the annual figures. Exports to the EEC from all the major trading regions have also increased since 1957, as indicated by the figures in Table 6-2. United States exports rose about 45% from 1957 to 1967, while exports from the rest of Western Europe (EFTA) rose 81%.

Removal of internal tariffs has been accompanied by a vigorous expansion of trade within the Community. Although some of this trade was no doubt diverted from its former channels, the overall growth of the Community has been so great that total trade with the outside world also increased. Although we cannot be sure that trade with nonmember countries is as great as it would have been without an EEC, it is encouraging to find that creation of the Community has not actually decreased the trade of member nations with outside countries. The fear of trade diversion is still strong, however, and in specific products the exports of some countries have decreased in absolute value.

A. *Agriculture*

The Rome treaty provided for a common agricultural policy in the EEC, but it left the details to be worked out in the future. Some of the most anxious moments in the Community's early years have come during the continuing negotiations on agricultural policy. France has repeatedly threatened to pull out if action were not taken to settle agricultural issues by a stated deadline.

Prices of major crops are supported in all EEC countries through price-support schemes similar to those of the United States, with imports controlled by means of quotas and tariffs. Prior to union, the support prices varied greatly from country to

Table 6-2. Exports to the European Economic Community (Millions of Dollars)

Year	From EEC Nations	From the Rest of the World	Breakdown of Exports from the Rest of the World		
			From U.S.	From EFTA	From Other Nations
1957	7,880	16,170	3,860	3,830	8,480
1958	7,530	14,620	2,840	3,650	8,130
1963	15,920	22,610	4,860	6,070	11,680
1964	18,390	24,690	5,230	6,450	13,010
1965	20,820	25,850	5,200	6,780	13,870
1966	23,230	27,640	5,460	7,060	15,120
1967	24,510	28,100	5,610	6,950	15,540

Sources. United Nations, *Yearbook of International Trade Statistics, 1966;* United Nations, *Monthly Bulletin of Statistics,* March 1969.

country, being highest in Germany and Italy, lowest in France and the Netherlands, but all were above world market prices in all member countries.

Creation of the common market meant that all restrictions on agricultural trade within the Community must be removed, and choice of the Community-wide support price levels became a crucial issue both to member nations and the outside world. Under the common agricultural policy, farmers within the Community are allowed to produce as much as they wish at the agreed support price, with imports permitted only to meet any excess of demand over domestic production. Imports are subject to a "variable levy," a tariff that can be raised or lowered as required to admit only the desired amount of imports. With domestic producers guaranteed a fixed domestic price, their production plans can be stabilized; flexibility is provided by changes in import volume. Foreign producers of agricultural products have a very uncertain market with a variable levy in operation, as the following comment implies.

The variable import levy . . . is an absolutely protective device: it can be adjusted to meet daily market changes, and can be kept, at all times, sufficiently large to confine imports to the difference between domestic production at the support price and consumption at that price. Unlike a tariff, which foreign producers can climb over if they can get their prices down sufficiently, the variable levy cannot be surmounted because the levy will automatically rise if foreign prices fall.[5]

The main issues in the controversy over agriculture can best be seen in the case of grains. All member nations produce the major grains—wheat, barley, rye, and corn—but the Community as a whole is a net importer. In the period from 1957 to 1959, the EEC produced about 50.5 million tons of grains annually, consumed 59.8 million tons, and thus had *net* imports of 9.3 million tons, of which about one half came from the United States. Within the Community, Germany and Italy are the principal importers, and their support prices were high in order to keep their small, inefficient farmers in business.[6] France, on the other hand, has a more efficient agriculture. French support prices were lower than the German and Italian prices, and France has the capacity to expand production considerably if demand were ensured.

The dispute about agriculture was sharpest between France and Germany. Germany wanted a *high* support price for grain in order to protect the livelihood of the large German farm population. The farm vote is large and German political leaders were extremely reluctant to do anything to offend the farmers. Germany also wanted to continue using quotas to shield its market from the more efficient French farmers. France wanted a *low* support price (but higher than world market prices) and, above all, the French insisted that complete free trade in agricultural products had to prevail within the Community. Under these conditions, French agricultural production would expand, and France would export grain to the rest of the Community, especially to Germany. The small, high-cost German farmer would be forced out of business. This result is one of the expected effects of free trade—a reallocation of resources in the trading countries. The adjustment looked easy in the examples

[5] *Trade Negotiations for a Better Free World Economy*, Committee for Economic Development, May 1964, p. 27.
[6] Italy's support price was high for wheat, but low for the coarse grains used for animal feed.

in Chapter 2, when German wheat production was made to shrink, releasing resources to the expanding steel industry, but in the short run the adjustment is painful and difficult. The traditions and the very lives of a great many people are affected by the changes that free trade requires.

A compromise was finally reached in December 1963, just a few days before General de Gaulle's ultimatum expired. Germany accepted the principle of a common agricultural policy, with Community-wide support prices and complete elimination of national restrictions on the movement of agricultural products within the Community. Several support prices were set, but the crucial issue of a common support price for grain was postponed until after the forthcoming German elections. Finally, in December 1964, the Council of Ministers agreed on a common target price for grains. For soft wheat, the common price was set at $106 per metric ton, somewhat closer to the French price of $100 than to the German price of $119 per ton. The common grain prices did not go into effect until July 1968, thus providing a further transition period. In addition, compensatory payments were provided for farmers injured by the abrupt price adjustment. Most compensatory payments were to go to German and Italian farmers.

The French view thus prevailed on grain prices, but the compromise eased political pressure in Germany. It now seems likely that the EEC will become more nearly self-sufficient in agriculture. Support prices are high enough to induce an expansion in output in the agricultural regions, especially France, and the variable levy will operate to exclude imports as long as domestic output can satisfy demand. Technological advances in European agriculture are also operating in this direction. In fact, experience to date indicates that European production will exceed supply at present support levels. The financing of the resulting surpluses has already led to political problems.

Consequently, the prospect is for EEC agricultural imports to diminish—another example of trade diversion. Outside countries are well aware of this prospect, and they have been urging the EEC to take a more liberal position. They object especially to the variable levy because of its arbitrary and highly protectionist character. The stakes are large—EEC food imports were $6 billion in 1963—but there is little hope that the EEC policy will be altered.

Exchange rate changes made in 1969 have created internal problems for the EEC. Depreciation of the French franc made the common agricultural prices, which are set in terms of "units of account" (equal to the U.S. dollar), higher in terms of francs, while appreciation of the German mark had the opposite effect —it reduced the common agricultural prices in terms of marks. These exchange rate changes would thus tend to cause French production to expand and German production to decline. As it happened, the member nations were unwilling to allow the exchange rate changes to have their full effects upon agriculture, and action was taken to cushion the effect of both changes. French farmers were denied the full benefits of the franc depreciation, while German farmers were protected through a subsidy from the adverse effects of mark appreciation. In both cases the cushioning is supposed to be temporary, but this episode illustrates the problems caused by exchange rate changes within a common market.

B. *The European Free Trade Association*

When the first tentative moves toward European integration began in the 1950s, the British did not take them seriously. They participated in the negotiations, but they did not believe France and Germany would ever agree. However, when it became clear that the six member nations were, indeed, likely to form an economic union, the British moved to prevent the emergence of tariff discrimination within Europe and the resulting trade diversion. In 1956, they proposed the formation of a "free trade area" to embrace all OEEC countries.

In the proposed free-trade area, member countries would eliminate tariffs on trade among themselves, but each country would retain its own tariffs against the outside world. There would be no common external tariff. Nor did the proposal provide for the other aspects of an economic union—free movement of labor and capital, a common agricultural policy, or coordination of other economic and social policies. It was limited solely to trade. (The EEC could have gone ahead with its plans for full economic union, with its common external tariff. As a member of the proposed free-trade area, the EEC would simply not levy the common tariff on goods coming from other countries in the area.)

The British proposal was an ingenious attempt to avoid tariff discrimination within Europe, while leaving member countries free to set their own individual policies in other respects. It was tailored to fit British needs in several respects. The United Kingdom relied upon imports for most of its food and raw materials, and it wanted to continue to buy these at the lowest possible world market prices. The United Kingdom had a special relationship to the Commonwealth countries, including a system of tariff preferences. Such preferential tariffs could be retained in a free-trade area, but not in a common market such as the six member nations proposed. Above all, the United Kingdom shrank from the political implications of full economic union with continental Europe. The free-trade area proposal offered a middle course, but also a way to retain access to the important European market.

To be concise:[7] while negotiations on the British proposal dragged on in OEEC, the Treaty of Rome was signed (March 1957) and went into effect January 1, 1958; positions hardened; negotiations finally collapsed in November 1958; and Europe was split.

Having failed to achieve a free-trade area embracing all of Europe, the United Kingdom joined with six other OEEC countries (Norway, Sweden, Denmark, Austria, Switzerland, and Portugal) to form the European Free Trade Association. The treaty was signed in January 1960. The "Outer Seven," as they are called, reduced internal tariffs at about the same pace as the EEC, but they do not intend to set a common external tariff.[8]

---

[7] For a full account of this fascinating episode, see Miriam Camps, *Britain and the European Community, 1955–1963* (Princeton, 1964).

[8] When each nation retains its own external tariff, importers will naturally tend to import a commodity into that country whose tariff is lowest. Some trade distortion may therefore develop. To avoid it, EFTA has rules limiting internal free trade to commodities produced within the area, or commodities containing not more than 50% of imported materials, by value. This technical problem was a major issue in the negotiations for a free-trade area.

The hope was that the two groups could eventually be reconciled, so that trade could be free within all Europe.

Thus far, EFTA nations have not suffered severely from the trade diversion effect of the EEC. Indeed, EFTA exports to EEC nations rose from $3.8 billion in 1957 to $7.0 billion in 1967, as fast a rate of increase as in trade among EFTA countries themselves. However, there is still a strong fear that trade discrimination will be great when the EEC is in full operation.

This fear drove the United Kingdom to apply, in 1961, for full membership in the European Economic Community. If the United Kingdom had been admitted, the other EFTA members were expected to seek either full or associate membership, and the European split would be healed.[9] The British, at last, agreed to accept the common external tariff, to shift their agricultural policy to the European system, and to accept the wider implications of economic union. However, they hoped to obtain special treatment for certain Commonwealth countries, approximately as France had obtained special treatment in the Rome treaty for its African territories. The case of New Zealand was especially urgent, since the great bulk of its exports go to the United Kingdom. Numerous other problems arose during the long negotiations in 1961 and 1962, but many of them appeared to be in sight of solution when the British bid was torpedoed by General de Gaulle in January 1962. It is by no means certain that the British applications would have been successful, since the problems were great, but France did not want to risk it. Just as France had fooled the British by signing the Treaty of Rome, so the United Kingdom fooled the French by its decision to embrace even the political implications of full membership in the EEC. General de Gaulle decided it was time to use his veto.

In 1967, the United Kingdom renewed its bid to join the EEC. At first, it appeared that French objections to British entry were as strong as ever, but with the departure of General de Gaulle, the prospects of an acceptable compromise seem much brighter. In one sense, entry becomes more difficult as time passes—the

[9] In fact, Denmark applied for membership on the day after the British did; Ireland and Norway soon followed; and Austria, Sweden, and Switzerland applied for associate membership.

EEC will have settled a great many problems and the United Kingdom will have to accept these solutions, although if it had become a member in 1962 it would have had a hand in shaping the decisions. In the meantime, Europe is divided, and there is danger that the division may harden. Efforts are being made to keep some bridges open between the "Six" and the "Seven," and it may be that bilateral negotiations between these two groups will lessen the adverse effects to trade diversion in Europe itself.

III. ECONOMIC EFFECTS OF EUROPEAN INTEGRATION ON THE OUTSIDE WORLD

The chief fear of the outside world is that progress toward economic integration in Europe will cause massive trade diversion. In short, outside countries fear that their exports to EEC countries will be displaced. As we have seen, this effect has not yet occurred; rapid economic growth has caused an *increase* in EEC imports from the outside world. Trade creation appears to have outweighed trade diversion. The future may be different, however, and pessimists point to the following four factors which lead them to believe that trade diversion will be a serious threat in coming years.

First, the final steps toward a full customs union were not taken until 1968. Thus, the full impact of tariff discrimination against outside countries has only recently been felt. The first reductions in internal duties and the first moves toward a common external tariff were offset by removal of quotas and other nontariff restrictions, and by rapid growth in income, but these offsets will not be present to alleviate the impact of the final tariff changes.

Second, the EEC's common agricultural policy was not in operation in the first phase. Now that agreement has been reached on Community-wide support prices for major commodities, internal production will expand, and the variable-tariff system will begin to limit agricultural imports.

Third, the rise in EEC imports from the outside world has resulted, in large part, from the rapid increase in income in member countries—an increase that may not continue at the same pace in the future. It is significant that the fraction of each dollar of income spent for imports from the outside world has declined since 1957. This fraction, the "average propensity to import," declined from 11.0% in 1957 to 8.4% in 1966. Therefore, the "marginal propensity to import," the fraction of each *additional* dollar of income spent for imports, was only 6.5% in this period, 1957 to 1966.

Fourth, the role of "associated states" will grow in importance, with adverse effects on the outside world. To explain this point, we must first describe the "associate" relationship in more detail. When the Treaty of Rome was signed, France had close economic and political ties with a number of African countries and territories. Some of them were, under French law, a part of metropolitan France; they were incorporated as departments in the French Union. The other territories were also supposed to be integrated eventually into the French economy. France already had special trade arrangements with all of these territories. Their exports entered France duty free, and French goods were given preferences in their markets. France thus had a system of preferential tariffs similar to that between the United Kingdom and the Commonwealth.

France wanted to retain its special role in Africa, and the French government therefore stated that it would not join the EEC unless these African territories were included as "associated territories" with certain rights and privileges.[10] France won the point, and the Treaty of Rome provided that reductions in internal tariffs among the Six should also apply to imports from these associated countries and territories, but that they, in turn, were not required to eliminate *their* tariffs on imports from the Six.[11] Now that the customs union is in full operation, imports from these African countries will enter the EEC without tariffs, while their competitors in Asia and Latin America must pay the common external tariff.

[10] The pertinent articles in the Treaty of Rome are phrased in more general language, to include as associates the overseas territories of any of the six signatories, but these French territories were the chief ones affected.
[11] The Rome treaty also provides for a development fund to be used for economic development in the African territories, but it does not provide for the free movement of workers between the EEC and Africa. This matter is left for future negotiation.

Since the African associates are, actually or potentially, important producers of tropical foodstuffs such as coffee, sugar, cocoa, and bananas, and since the common external tariff rates were originally quite high on some products, the threat to exporters in the outside world is very great. They may yet suffer substantial loss of export markets as trade is diverted to the associated states. The countries that stand to lose are mostly underdeveloped countries, including some in Africa itself who do not have the status of associates—for example, Ghana and Nigeria. These countries are acutely aware of the discriminatory effect of the EEC, and they have vigorously resisted it. At least partly as a result of their protests, the EEC has reduced its external tariff targets on some of the affected commodities. For example, the planned tariff on coffee has been cut from 16 to 9% and that on cocoa from 9 to 5%.

The associated overseas countries, mostly former French territories, include the following.

Burundi	Mali
Cameroon	Mauretania
Central African Republic	Niger
Chad	Rwanda
Congo	Senegal
Dahomey	Somali Republic
Gabon	Togo
Ivory Coast	Upper Volta
Malagasy	

These new countries cover a sparsely settled area larger than the United States.

There is still another aspect of the problem of association that we must mention. The Rome treaty also provided that any country, in Europe or elsewhere, might become associated with the EEC by negotiating an agreement specifying the terms of the association. This provision is very broad, and could permit a wide variety of associate relationships. Greece and Turkey have already become associated countries under this clause. Greece will adopt the common external tariff, and most of its goods will enter the EEC free of duty, but Greece is given a lengthy transition period (up to 22 years) in which to remove its tariffs on imports from the EEC. The agreement with Turkey is tailored to fit Turkey's special problems, but it also looks toward eventual full integration of Turkey into the EEC. Several other countries have applied for association or sought to negotiate special agreements with the EEC under this provision in the treaty. These countries include the following ones.

Austria
Israel
Spain
Nigeria
Kenya
India
Iran

For all of these reasons, many observers fear that the discriminatory bite of the EEC tariff structure will increase in the future, and that serious trade diversion away from outside countries and toward member nations and associated states will occur. This fear is increased by signs of protectionist sentiment in the EEC.

A major objective of foreign trade policy in the United States and other outside countries has been to lessen the severity of such trade diversion. It is not an exaggeration to say that the primary purpose of the United States' Trade Expansion Act of 1962 was to provide ways to offset the discriminatory character of the European common market. That Act, passed in the summer of 1962 when British entry into the EEC appeared likely, contained three major provisions. The President was empowered to do the following things.

1. To decrease any tariff rate by 50% of the rate existing on July 1, 1962.

2. To reduce to *zero* the tariff on any article for which the combined exports of the United States and the EEC accounts for 80% of total free world exports.

3. To reduce to *zero* the tariffs on tropical foods and forestry products if the EEC did the same.

The Act also contained escape clauses, exceptions, and provisions for compensation and assistance to workers and firms injured by tariff reductions, but we shall not describe these in detail.

Our interest lies in the ingenious attempt made to offset tariff discrimination in the EEC and, at the same time, to hold out a helping hand to underdeveloped countries. If the United Kingdom had become a member of EEC, the other EFTA nations would have quickly followed. The combined exports of the United States and the expanded EEC would then have constituted 80% or more of a long list of manufactured goods. Under the Trade Expansion Act, we could have joined with the EEC to eliminate tariffs on these goods, thus creating a free-trade area in the entire Atlantic community. Under GATT rules, these tariff reductions would also be extended to the rest of the free world (the underdeveloped countries) by virtue of the most-favored-nations clause. Consequently, underdeveloped countries would have obtained free access to advanced country markets for their exports of manufactured goods, but they would not themselves have had to make reciprocal concessions. As we saw in Chapter 5, that was one of their major policy objectives, as stated at the United Nations Conference on Trade and Development.

Unfortunately, this key provision in the Trade Expansion Act was emasculated by the French veto on British entry. Without Britain, only a few commodities qualify under the 80% rule. The entire scheme collapses. General de Gaulle clearly stated his dislike of the concept of a "colossal Atlantic community" embracing both Western Europe and the United States; the Trade Expansion Act may well have influenced his decision to block the British bid to join the EEC.

Presidential power to eliminate duties on tropical foods and forestry products also depended on similar action by the EEC. This provision was not rendered meaningless by the failure of British entry, but since United States duties were already zero on many tropical products, we had little leverage to persuade the EEC to eliminate its high duties on these products. This problem is accentuated by the presence of the associated countries, which now have a vested interest in keeping a high common external tariff on the products they export to the common market.

Consequently, the main thrust of the Trade Expansion Act depended on the first provision on our list—the power to reduce tariffs 50% in exchange for reciprocal concessions from other nations. At the beginning of the so-called "Kennedy Round" of tariff negotiations, the United States proposed a 50% tariff reduction across the board, with exceptions only for essential defense industries and cases of severe hardship. The requirement of full reciprocity meant that the EEC would have to reduce its common external tariff by the same proportion. When the United States negotiators advanced this proposal, the EEC negotiators objected, arguing that an equal percentage cut was not really an equal exchange when the two tariff structures were considered. Their point was that the United States tariff still includes many high rates in excess of 50%, while EEC tariff rates clustered in the 0 to 20% range with very few rates above 30%. If the United States reduced a duty of, for example, 90% by one half, the remaining level of protection (45%) would still be high. But if the EEC cut a 20% tariff in half, the remaining 10% tariff would have very little protective effect. Therefore, the EEC negotiators argued that the United States should lop off its peak rates, since only then would equal, across-the-board tariff reductions really represent a fair exchange.

This "tariff disparities" argument was rather disconcerting to the United States negotiators, who first thought it a French ploy to sabotage the Kennedy round. United States hopes had been high because Congress had, for the first time, authorized across-the-board reductions; previously the United States had been required to negotiate on an item-by-item basis with many commodities exempted, and the negotiating process had been unwieldy. Furthermore, in the 1961 GATT negotiations (the "Dillon round"), the EEC itself had offered a 20% reduction across the board. At that time the United States had been unable to bargain on that basis, and the Trade Expansion Act of 1962 had been deliberately designed to permit across-the-board cuts.

As a matter of fact, United States tariff rates *are* spread out over a wider range than EEC rates. The United States has a larger percentage of *low* duties (under 5%), but also a larger percentage of *high* duties (over 30%). For example, one study found that 26.4% of United States tariff rates were below 5%, and

9.7% were above 30%.[12] Corresponding figures for the EEC were 16% and 1.4%. Therefore, the French insistence on "lopping off the peaks" had some basis in fact.

It is difficult to compare average levels of tariffs in two different customs areas, and even more difficult to compare their protective effects. Numerous efforts have been made to compare the United States and EEC tariffs, however, and we shall report a few results. In one study an unweighted average of tariff rates was calculated, using the same commodity classifications for both areas. The overall tariff average turned out to be virtually identical: 13.9% for the United States and 14.0% for the EEC.[13] Within the total, EEC tariffs were considerably higher than United States tariffs on food, beverages, and tobacco (17.8 to 8.5%), while United States tariffs were slightly higher than EEC tariffs on other products (15.2 to 13.2%). When tariffs are weighted by the value of imports of each commodity, all of the averages decline substantially. The overall averages remain similar—7.6% for the United States and 8.3% for the EEC. Weighting by import value tends to bias the average downward, of course, since a tariff so high as to be prohibitive (for instance, 200%) would have *no* effect on the average because the value of imports would be zero and the high tariff would have no weight. In 1964 the EEC calculated an unweighted tariff average, *excluding* agricultural products, and found the average for the EEC common external tariff to be 11.7% against 17.8% for the United States.[14]

All of the above comparisons are based on nominal tariff rates, but many economists argue that comparisons based on "effective tariff" rates are more relevant (see p. 103 for the definition). Balassa's calculations indicate that average levels of effective duties are quite similar in the U.S. and the EEC; for all manufactured products, he obtained average effective tariffs of 20% in

[12] *Trade Negotiations for a Better Free World Economy,* op cit.
[13] *Trade Negotiations for a Better Free World Economy,* op. cit., Appendix B.
[14] Cited in Randall Hinshaw, *The European Economic Community and American Trade* (New York, 1964), pp. 80-81. Chapter 5 contains a useful summary of Atlantic tariff comparisons.

the U.S. and 18.6% in the EEC.[15] These averages conceal large differences in tariff rates on particular products, however.

In general, it seems safe to say that United States tariffs are lower than EEC tariffs on food (although both areas use quotas and other nontariff restrictions to keep out foodstuffs that are competitive with domestic producers), but higher on manufactures than EEC tariffs. However, on many specific manufactures, EEC tariffs are higher than the United States. For example, the EEC tariff on automobiles is 22%, the United States tariff only 6 1/2% (by 1972 these rates will be reduced to 11% and 3% respectively). In both areas, tariffs on raw materials are very low, with many goods admitted free of duty.

Although the Trade Expansion Act was passed in 1962, the Kennedy Round of tariff negotiations did not end until June 1967. The results achieved in these marathon sessions were impressive, even if less than had been hoped. Fifty-three nations were parties to the agreements, and thousands of products were involved, accounting for about $40 billion of world trade. On the average, tariffs on nonagricultural goods were cut by about 35%, but on many products the full 50% cut was achieved. These cuts are to be made in five equal stages and completed by January 1, 1972. Most nations agreed to make the cuts on January 1 of each year, beginning in 1968, but the EEC chose to make the first two cuts at once on July 1, 1968. Underdeveloped countries did not participate very actively in the negotiations, and they made few concessions, although they did "bind" some tariffs (i.e., promise not to raise them). They also benefited, through the most-favored-nation clause, from the tariff cuts made by advanced countries.

The Kennedy Round negotiators also made a small but useful beginning on the thorny problem of nontariff barriers to trade. One of these, the U.S. practice of valuation of certain chemicals on the basis of their "American selling price" (ASP), became a major bone of contention in the negotiations. Europeans object to the ASP valuation because it increases the actual amount of tariff charged on their chemical exports to the United States. A

[15] Bela Balassa, *Trade Liberalization Among Industrial Countries* (New York: McGraw Hill, 1967), p. 56.

compromise was finally reached under which some of the European tariff reductions on chemicals were made contingent upon elimination of the ASP valuation system by the United States—a step which requires an act of Congress.

One prime objective of United States policy is to retain access for American agricultural exports in the European market, but tariff bargaining is not well suited to cope with the common agricultural policy in the EEC. As we have mentioned, the variable levy is an absolutely protective device. Since it is variable, one cannot bargain to reduce it by a given percentage. The United States (and other outside countries) have therefore urged the EEC to allow imports of agricultural products to retain their historic share in the market. "Historic share" usually means the share held in the last years before adoption of the common agricultural policy. The EEC has made no promises as yet, but the French are likely to demand that their farmers be allowed free rein to expand output at the common support prices. That policy, plus continued advances in agricultural technology, will probably make the EEC more nearly self-sufficient in food.

The United States has a strong comparative advantage in agriculture, and EEC nations have been an important export market, but the outlook is gloomy for United States agricultural exports. This issue was dramatized in 1963 by the famous "chicken war" between the United States and the EEC. During the last few years, technological changes in poultry raising in the United States greatly reduced the cost of production and the prices of chickens, turkeys, and other poultry products. Since the price of feed grains is considerably higher in Europe than in the United States, this factor plus the new technology caused a rapid increase in United States exports of poultry products to Europe. In Germany, for example, United States exports brought such a fall in poultry prices that per capita consumption rose from about 4 to 13 pounds per year.[16] The German tariff on poultry was 15%, a barrier that the United States exports could easily surmount. Then, in 1962, the EEC adopted a common agricultural policy on poultry which required the use of variable levies

---

[16] Finn Jensen and Ingo Walter, *The Common Market: Economic Integration in Europe* (New York, 1965), 231.

on imports from outside countries. The result was a sharp increase in protection and an abrupt fall in United States poultry exports. In early 1965, the German import levy was 64% against 15% prior to adoption of the common policy. The United States vigorously protested this increased tariff, correctly arguing that it was a violation of the GATT provision that a customs union should not increase the average level of protection that existed in member countries prior to union. When the EEC refused to alter its policy, the United States retaliated by increasing its tariffs on several EEC products, including trucks, wine, film, and cheese.

The United States and the EEC have not even been able to agree on a basis for negotiation with respect to agriculture. The United States wants to bargain about the share of imports in the European market; but the EEC wants to bargain about the "margin of support" afforded agriculture.

The general view is that the EEC attitude has changed since 1962, and that it has become more inward-looking, more protectionist in outlook. This change has been led by the French, and it may indicate the strength of French influence in the Community. The French position may stem primarily from political issues, but we should note that membership in the EEC itself requires a large reduction in French tariffs against the outside world. This reduction occurs because French tariffs were originally higher than the Community average and, consequently, the movement toward a common external tariff meant a net reduction in the French tariff level. (Germany, on the other hand, ended with *more* tariff protection against nonmember countries than it had before the Rome treaty.) In addition, France also eliminated tariffs on imports from other members. All of this has been a rough jolt to French industries—long accustomed to a sheltered domestic market. No wonder France has wanted to slow the pace of economic integration in recent years.

7

World Payments Problem

I. BALANCE-OF-PAYMENTS ADJUSTMENT
WITH FIXED EXCHANGE RATES

When a nation has a deficit in its balance of payments, it draws down its foreign exchange reserves, loses gold, or incurs short-term liabilities.[1] A properly functioning international monetary system must provide some means to put an end to such a deficit. That is, the system must include a "mechanism of adjustment," a process through which equilibrium in the balance of payments can be restored. The principal flaw in the present international monetary system is that nations are not willing and able to accept the adjustment mechanism that it implies. They act to block the corrective process or to slow it, and as a result deficits tend to last a long time. However, deficits *must* be terminated, one way or another, because the deficit nation will eventually run out of gold and foreign exchange reserves, and other nations are not willing to extend unlimited credit. The question is *how* the deficit will be corrected: whether by an orderly, systematic process, or by a series of emergency actions in each case.

[1] The term "deficit in the balance of payments" was defined in Chapter 4. The reader should review that section. Briefly, a deficit exists when a nation's payments to the outside world for goods and services (A), gifts and transfers (B), and purchases of long-term assets (C) exceed its receipts from the outside world for these three items. The deficit nation makes up the difference by drawing on its stock of gold and foreign currencies, or by borrowing short-term funds.

Exchange-rate change is one powerful method that could be used to correct a deficit, but most nations are extremely reluctant to use it, especially the advanced industrial nations of the Atlantic community. Therefore, we shall concentrate on the problem of balance-of-payments adjustment in a system of fixed exchange rates. Economists have long had a theory to explain the adjustment process with fixed exchange rates. The theory was stated quite clearly by David Hume in the 18th century, but it has since been expanded and somewhat modified. People still speak of the "classical" adjustment process, however.

To explain this theory, we shall continue an example that was begun in Chapter 4. Suppose that the United Kingdom has a deficit in its balance of payments at the official par value of the pound sterling, £1.0 = $2.40. The initial situation is dipicted in Figure

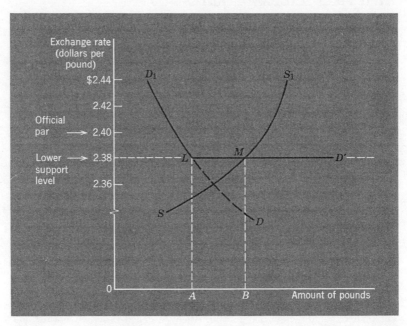

Figure 7-1. Dollar-sterling exchange rate. The supply of pounds exceeds demand at the official par exchange rate, $2.40 = £1. Therefore, the price of the pound falls. When it reaches the lower support level, $2.38, the United Kingdom Stabilization Fund buys up the excess supply of pounds, $LM \ (= AB)$.

7-1, a reproduction of Figure 4-1 (Chapter 4). The excess supply of pounds at the official par value causes the market rate to drop to the lower limit, £1.0 = $2.38, where it is supported by the United Kingdom Stabilization Fund. (As explained in Chapter 4, this support is a responsibility of the United Kingdom under the rules of the International Monetary Fund.) The United Kingdom Stabilization Fund buys up the excess pounds, paying for them out if its stock of United States dollars. In Figure 7-1 the deficit measured in pounds is *LM*, or *AB*.

When the Stabilization Fund buys *LM* of pounds, the action reduces bank reserves and demand deposits of London banks. Money becomes tighter. The banks must be stricter about making new loans, and they may have to reduce the total amount of outstanding loans. The central bank, the Bank of England, will probably raise the "bank rate"—the rate of interest that it charges on loans and discounts to the money market. ("Bank rate" is similar to the rediscount rate" of the Federal Reserve System.) A rise in the bank rate causes a rise in short-term interest rates in London, and some short-term funds may be attracted to the London money market. For example, when the interest rate on United Kingdom 90-day Treasury bills rises, American firms and individuals tend to buy more of them. Therefore, the demand for pounds increases; in our diagram the original demand curve for pounds (D_1) shifts to the right, to D_2, as shown in Figure 7-2. This increased private demand for pounds relieves the pressure on the exchange rate and reduces the amount of pounds that the Stabilization Fund must buy to support the exchange rate. Indeed, if the disturbance is only a temporary one, these changes in short-term interest rates may be all that is needed. In an earlier era, especially the period before the First World War, changes in "bank rate" had a powerful effect upon the flow of short-term capital, and "this marvelous and beautiful instrument" of economic policy played an important role in preserving equilibrium in the United Kingdom balance of payments.

If the deficit is more than a temporary disturbance, however, changes in bank rate may not be enough to correct it. More fundamental adjustments will be needed. They are supposed to occur through the effect on national income and prices of a long-continued tight-money policy. As bank reserves and the money

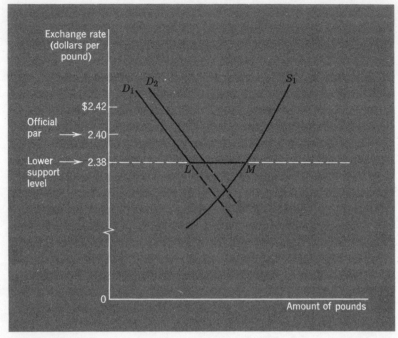

Figure 7-2. Short-run adjustment. The rise in short-term interest rates in London causes a shift in the demand for pounds, from D_1 to D_2, as foreigners move funds to London to take advantage of the higher interest rates.

supply fall, credit tightens and long-term interest rates rise. Higher interest rates tend to reduce expenditures for investment, both public and private, and for durable consumer goods. Thus a local government may postpone a bond issue to finance a new school or road; a corporation may decide not to build a new plant; and many families may decide not to build a new house because monthly mortgage payments have increased. All of these decisions to cancel or postpone expenditures will, when added together, constitute a significant decrease in total investment. As investment falls, incomes fall in capital goods industries. Those whose incomes fall then reduce *their* expenditures for consumption, further reducing incomes elsewhere, and thus through the familiar multiplier process the national income of the deficit country is reduced. A direct decline in expenditure may also occur because of a shift in world demand from domestic to foreign goods.

The fall in money income and gross national product may be accompanied by a fall in the prices of many products. Some prices and wages may be sticky, but a fall in GNP is likely to cause downward pressure on prices even when unions are strong and firms are shy about engaging in vigorous price competition.

These effects are supposed to take place more or less automatically as a result of changes in reserves and the money supply. Such deflationary pressure might be augmented by deliberate fiscal policy—the government could increase tax rates, thus reducing disposable income of the population, or it could curtail its own expenditures for goods and services.

As money incomes and prices fall in the deficit country, its demand for imports tends to fall, while its exports may rise. Imports fall for two reasons.

First, as money incomes fall, people reduce their expenditures for all goods and services, including imported goods and services. There is a positive relationship between national income and imports—when income rises, imports rise; when income falls, imports fall. The ratio of the change in imports to the change of income $(\Delta M/\Delta Y)$ is the "marginal propensity to import." The size of this ratio varies from country to country, but it is positive in all. In the United Kingdom, the marginal propensity to import is about 20%, in the Netherlands about 50% and the United States about 5%. The higher the ratio, the more efficient is a decline in income in correcting a current-account deficit.

Second, as the prices of domestic goods fall, some consumers substitute cheaper domestic goods for imported goods. In practice, the decline of imports caused by the switch from imports to home goods because of price changes is mixed up with the decline in imports because of falling income. Analytically, we can speak of an "income effect" and a "price effect," but statistically they are difficult to distinguish. Exports rise because foreigners also find United Kingdom goods more attractive as their prices fall, and they tend to substitute United Kingdom goods for their own products. Foreign incomes may also be rising, causing a rise in *their* imports.

These changes in income and prices are accompanied by shifts in the demand and supply of pounds in the foreign exchange

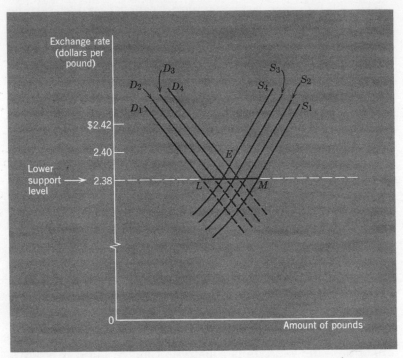

Figure 7-3. Longer-run adjustment. As the levels of income and prices are forced down in the United Kingdom, additional shifts in the demand and supply of pounds occur. Demand shifts to the right, to D_2, D_3, D_4, as United Kingdom goods become cheaper to foreign buyers; supply shifts to the left, to S_2, S_3, S_4, as United Kingdom citizens reduce their purchases of imports.

market. The supply curve shifts to the left, as shown in Figure 7-3, representing a decline in supply as United Kingdom incomes fall and expenditures are switched from imports to domestic goods as domestic prices fall. The demand curve shifts to the right, representing an increase in foreign demand for United Kingdom goods as they become cheaper. Both of these shifts reduce the size of the United Kingdom deficit, and when the changes in income and prices have gone far enough to eliminate it, the exchange rate will rise above the lower support level, and the Stabilization Fund will no longer need to buy pounds. The excess supply of pounds will have been eliminated by corrective changes in interest rates, incomes, and prices. This situation is depicted in Figure 7-3, with the final demand curve (D_4) and supply curve (S_4) intersecting at E. The initial deficit has been removed.

In this description of the adjustment process, we have concentrated on what happens in the *deficit* country. Opposite changes are supposed to occur in the surplus country, thus reducing the severity of deflationary pressures in the deficit country. That is, the surplus country, which is gaining reserves, should increase its money supply, lower interest rates, and allow its national income and price level to rise. Such expansion would increase its demand for imports, thus causing an increase in the demand for pounds in our example. In practice, however, the surplus country often counteracts the expansionary influence of its surplus, and leaves the main burden of adjustment on the deficit country. The adjustment process is asymmetrical in this sense, that the deficit country absolutely must correct its deficit, while the surplus country may enjoy its surplus position and feel no pressure to end it.

The traditional adjustment process requires the deficit country to accept some deflationary pressure, to allow interest rates to rise and prices and money wages to fall. This "classical medicine" has obvious political implications, and it may, in fact, be so unpopular that the deficit country will reject it. In the modern world, money wages are not easily reduced, and a reduction in aggregate demand is likely to cause unemployment. No government wants to let unemployment and a domestic recession be dictated by external influences—by a balance-of-payment deficit. Such subordination of domestic economic policy to the requirements of the external balance has been unpopular since the Great Depression, and one goal of the International Monetary Fund was to enable member nations to fix their domestic economic policies to suit themselves. As John Maynard Keynes said in 1945:

We are determined that . . . the external value of sterling shall conform to its internal value as set by our own domestic policies, and not the other way round. Secondly, we intend to retain control of our domestic rate of interest, so that we can keep it as low as suits our own purposes. . . . Thirdly, whilst we intend to prevent inflation at home, we shall not accept deflation at the dictate of influences from outside. In other words, we abjure the instruments of bank rate and credit contraction operating through the increase of unemployment as a means of forcing our domestic economy into line with external factors.[2]

In practice, however, nations have been reluctant to change their exchange rates, and domestic policy has had to bend to suit the external requirements. In Keynes' own country, the United Kingdom, the bank rate was raised to 7% in 1961 and to 8% in 1969 to combat an external deficit.

Nevertheless, the reluctance to make vigorous use of the classical medicine has emphasized the need for large amounts of international reserves. When a nation has large reserves, it can finance a payments deficit for a long period of time. Large reserves do not *correct* a deficit, but they do provide a breathing spell. It is always possible that autonomous economic changes will bring a swing in favor of the deficit country, removing the deficit without the bitter medicine. For example, world consumers may change their tastes and develop a preference for the deficit country's goods, entrepreneurs in the deficit country may achieve a cost-reducing technological breakthrough that will stimulate exports, or the deficit country may be rescued by rising prices in other countries while it holds its own price level stable.

If it is not rescued by some such fortuitous circumstance, the deficit country must eventually take steps to curb its deficit. Even so, it may still reject the classical adjustment process. Nations have used much energy and ingenuity in a search for other ways to get rid of a deficit, ways more palatable than deflation and unemployment. Economists argue that the differences are more apparent than real, that the final effects of any measures to correct the deficit are fundamentally similar, but the political impact of the various measures may be very different.

Economists say that any measures taken to improve a nation's current account—that is, its transactions in goods and services—must be either *expenditure-reducing* or *expenditure-switching*. That is, if a nation's current account balance (exports minus im-

---

2 From his speech to the House of Lords, urging ratification of the charter of the International Monetary Fund. Reprinted in Seymour Harris, *The New Economics* (New York: Knopf, 1952), p. 374.

ports) is to rise, measures must be taken to reduce domestic expenditures, thereby reducing imports directly through the marginal propensity to import, or to switch expenditures away from imports and toward domestically produced goods. The classical medicine combines these two. The check to investment and the induced decline in consumption are expenditure-reducing, while the fall in prices tends to cause expenditures to be switched from imports onto home goods in the deficit country. (In the surplus country, expenditures tend to switch from its home goods to imports, which are the exports of the deficit country.)

Depreciation of the exchange rate is an expenditure-switching policy change. It raises import prices to buyers in the deficit country and lowers export prices to buyers in the outside world. A tariff is also an expenditure-switching policy. In 1964, the United Kingdom decided against a depreciation of the pound, but imposed a 15% tariff surcharge on nearly all imports in an effort to improve its trade balance. The tariff was similar in economic effect to a depreciation of the pound, but the political difference was considerable, both at home and abroad. (In 1967, the United Kingdom did depreciate the pound—by about 14%.)

Nations seem to prefer expenditure-switching policies to expenditure-reducing ones, although they resist the most effective switching policy: exchange-rate change. It is the deflationary aspects of expenditure-reducing policies that they object to. Besides tariffs, the expenditure-switching policies that nations have used include import quotas, exchange controls, subsidies to domestic producers competing with imports, laws requiring government agencies to buy at home (for example, the "buy-American" clause in United States law, which requires Federal agencies to buy domestically produced goods unless their prices exceed foreign prices by more than a given margin, recently 6%), and laws requiring that economic aid and loans to foreigners be spent in the lending country (so-called "tied aid" and "tied loans").

Unfortunately, however, expenditure-switching policies alone may not solve the problem. If a country has a deficit because its prices are out of line, policies that cause expenditures to be switched from imports to domestic goods will simply increase the demand for domestic goods and put more upward pressure on domestic prices. If domestic prices rise further as a result of the switch in expenditure, the balance of payments will tend to worsen again. To have much chance of success in eliminating a balance of payments deficit, an expenditure-switching policy must, at least, be accompanied by enough expenditure reduction to remove the inflationary aspect.

II. GOLD AND THE DOLLAR: AN ATLANTIC PROBLEM

The gravest problem faced by the international monetary system in recent years has been the series of United States balance-of-payments deficits beginning in 1958. So large, stubborn, and persistent have these deficits been that they have shaken the foundations of the system. Many experts have called for basic reforms, but nations have had difficulty in reaching agreement on what form these should take.

A. *Nature of the Problem*

When the United States runs a deficit, the amount of dollars offered for sale in the foreign exchange market exceeds the amount of dollars demanded. There is an excess supply of dollars, and other currencies tend to rise in price in terms of dollars. As we saw in Chapter 4, it is the responsibility of each member nation in the International Monetary Fund to stabilize the exchange rate between its currency and the dollar at the official par value, or within 1% of it. Consequently, when an excess supply of dollars is offered in the foreign exchange markets for marks, francs, lira, and other currencies, it is these nations (Germany, France, Italy, etc.) that must intervene in the market, buying up the excess supply of dollars and paying out their own national currencies. Under the IMF arrangements, the United States is the only nation that does not have a direct responsibility for stabilizing an exchange rate. The special position of the United States stems from the role of the dollar as a key currency. When other nations intervene, they, of course, increase their holdings of United States dollars, and they may acquire more than they wish to hold.

For its part, the United States has agreed, in the IMF Charter, to buy and sell gold at the fixed price of $35 per ounce[3] to all

---

[3] Actually, the buying price is $34.9125 and the selling price is $35.0875, but this small spread has little economic significance.

official holders, namely central banks and treasuries. When foreigners accumulate dollars, they therefore have the right to use these dollars to buy gold from the United States treasury at the fixed price. The dollar tie to gold is unique; no other country in the world today has committed itself to buy and sell gold at a fixed price.

As long as the United States gold stock was very large in relation to the dollar holdings of other countries, we did not sell much gold. Just after the Second World War the United States had two thirds of the world's stock of monetary gold, and other countries were desperately short of foreign exchange reserves, especially dollars. Therefore, when the United States began to run a small deficit in the 1950s, the flow of dollars was welcomed and gladly held by the recipient nations.

Beginning in 1958, however, the modest United States deficits suddenly became large and alarming. In 1958 to 1960 the deficit hovered around $4 billion, and a few countries, mainly in Europe, found themselves in the unaccustomed position of having to buy more dollars than they wished to hold. As foreign dollar holdings grew, and as it became clear that United States efforts to reduce the deficit were not succeeding, the ability of the United States to redeem in gold came into question. Some countries began to ask for gold in exchange for their dollars, and the United States gold stock steadily declined. It fell from $22.8 billion in 1957 to $10.4 billion at the end of 1968, and in the same period official foreign holdings of dollars rose from $9.4 to $15.5 billion.[4] (Dollar holdings of unofficial foreigners rose from $5.7 to $20.1 billion). Thus the total of potential claims came to exceed the value of our gold stock.

As foreign-owned dollar balances grew and the United States gold stock fell, the United States was faced with a classic "crisis of confidence." Doubts about the dollar were heightened by the continuing large deficits in our balance of payments, deficits that persisted even after the United States government began to take vigorous measures to reduce them. Rumors spread that the United States would raise the price of gold, as it had done in 1933.

---

[4] *Federal Reserve Bulletin*, February 1969. The figure for official dollar balances includes balances of international organizations.

Table 7-1. Changes in World Gold Reserves, 1965 to 1967 (Millions of Dollars)

	1965	1966	1967
Production	$1,440	$1,440	$1,410
Soviet bloc sales [purchases(−)]	400	−75	−5
Total new supply	$1,840	$1,365	$1,405
Industrial consumption and private hoarding	−1,630	−1,410	−2,985
Net addition to monetary gold stocks [reduction (−)]	210	−45	−1,580

Source. *Annual Report, 1968, International Monetary Fund.*

Speculators rushed to buy gold, and in 1960 the price of gold rose to $40 per ounce in the London gold market, a free market in which both individuals and governments could deal.[5] The price subsequently fell back to about $35 per ounce as the United States reaffirmed its determination to hold the price at that level. A group of central banks agreed to supply gold to the London market whenever the price there rose over $35.20. This arrangement worked fairly well from 1961 to 1966, although it did expose the world's stock of monetary gold to private demand. Until 1967, at least a part of the newly produced gold went into monetary stocks (about 40%, on average), but in 1967 a heavy private demand for gold exceeded new production by $1.5 billion and thus drained that much gold out of central banks (see Table 7-1).

This sharp increase in speculative demand for gold led central bankers to devise a scheme that was designed to cut the link between monetary gold stocks and private holdings, and to establish a two-price system for gold. Beginning in March 1968, the United States announced that it would buy and sell gold *only* in transactions with central banks and monetary authorities, and that the price would remain $35 per ounce in this official market. Other central banks agreed that they would neither buy nor sell any gold except in transactions with other monetary authorities. If

[5] United States law prohibits United States' citizens from buying or owning gold, either at home or abroad, but some countries permit private ownership of gold.

all monetary authorities were to abide by this arrangement, the world's monetary gold stock would remain fixed, and official transactions would take place at $35 per ounce.

In the private gold markets, price would depend on demand and supply. Since *all* newly produced gold must be disposed of in this market, if speculative demand were to subside the price would drop below the official price. Needless to say, South Africa, the world's largest producer, strongly opposed this two-price system. South Africa has so far (Dec. 1969) refused to sell gold in the free market, except for small amounts allegedly sold through Swiss banks, but has instead let its current production accumulate in the hope that the central bank agreement will be eroded. After March 1968 the price of gold fluctuated widely; it reached a high of $49 per ounce, but in late 1969 the price dropped back to $35 as the new facility for "Special Drawing Rights" in the IMF received final approval (see Sect. IV, below).

Despite the United States' pledge to keep the official price of gold unchanged, some central banks remained uneasy about their large dollar balances, and they continued to convert some of these dollars into gold. The reason central banks were uneasy is that if the United States suddenly raised the price of gold, for instance, from $35 to $70 per ounce, a central bank holding dollars would suffer a 50% loss in terms of gold while any central bank holding gold would double the value of its reserve in terms of dollars. Central bankers have long memories, and they have not forgotten losses suffered in 1931, when Britain went off gold, and in 1933, when the United States raised the price of gold about 70%.

The fundamental difficulty in the international monetary system, as Robert Triffin has emphasized, is that nations must hold their international reserves either in gold or in *national currencies*. The system provides no other alternative (but see Section IV, below). However, increments to the world's monetary gold stock from newly mined gold are not large enough to supply the desired increases in reserves; hence the necessity to increase the amount of reserves held in national currencies. The United States dollar and the United Kingdom pound are the two currencies that have served most widely as a reserve medium for other countries, but both of them have been under a cloud in recent years. A flight from these two "key currencies" into gold would seriously weaken the present system because it would reduce the national-currency component of international reserves and thus reduce the total amount of reserves in the system, and because it could exhaust the United States gold stock and force us to break the link between gold and the dollar.

One trouble is that the world's output of newly mined gold is not large enough to supply the needed additions to international reserves. Although current output has been supplemented in some recent years by Soviet sales in the London gold market, over one half of the total new supply has been absorbed by industrial uses or has gone into private hoards. Table 7-1 contains figures for 1965 to 1967; it may be seen that only in 1965 was any net addition made to mounting gold reserves. Under the present system, any other increase in world monetary reserves must take the form of national currencies. Of all currencies, the United States dollar is most widely accepted for this purpose, but as we have seen, it too has become suspect because of the large, apparently uncontrollable United States deficits.

Note that this problem of reserve adequacy and confidence in the dollar is largely limited to the Atlantic community; it is European nations that are accumulating dollars and arousing fears about the adequacy of the United States gold stock by converting dollars into gold. The reserves of underdeveloped nations in Asia, Africa, and Latin America have not risen appreciably, nor have their holdings of gold increased. Table 7-2 contains some figures to illustrate this point. Gold held by the entire world, outside of OECD nations, changed very little from 1951 to 1968. Furthermore, as we saw in Chapter 5, it is most unlikely that underdeveloped countries will be able to accumulate much exchange reserves in the future. The pressures of their domestic development programs will require them to spend all available external funds on current purchases and debt service.

In fact, the demand for gold has come from a small group of surplus countries in Europe. Nearly all of the increase in gold stocks since 1958 has occurred in France, Germany, Italy, the Netherlands, Spain, and Switzerland. Other nations seem more willing to hold increments in their reserves in the form of dollars. It is in this sense that instability of the international monetary system is an *Atlantic* problem.

Table 7-2. Official Reserves of Gold and Foreign Exchange (Billions of United States Dollars)

	1951			1959			1968		
	Gold	Exchange	Total	Gold	Exchange	Total	Gold	Exchange	Total
Atlantic community[a]	7.4	4.5	11.9	14.0	9.7	23.7	22.9	14.1	37.0
Rest of world[b]	3.7	8.7	12.4	3.4	7.4	10.8	5.1	13.3	18.4
United States	22.9	—	22.9	20.6	—	20.6	10.9	3.5	14.4
Total	34.0	13.2	47.2	38.0	17.1	55.1	38.9	30.9	69.8

Source. International Financial Statistics, International Monetary Fund, April 1969.
[a] This includes all members of OECD, except the United States.
[b] This includes all nations outside the Soviet bloc except the members of OECD.

B. *The United States Response*

When the United States waked up, about 1960, and began to take its payments deficit seriously, it sought to stabilize domestic prices and wages, but it did not attempt to force them down. For one thing, the United States had an uncomfortably high rate of unemployment, and the government was extremely reluctant to apply deflationary pressure to an economy already suffering from 6 to 7% unemployment. Furthermore, to many people, it seemed foolish to force an economy with a GNP of $500 to $600 billion to contract in order to correct a balance-of-payments deficit of only $3 to $4 billion. To do so would be to let the tail wag the dog, it was said. The United States has such a low marginal propensity to import (about 5%) that income must fall $20 in order to bring about a fall of $1 in imports. Public concern about the low rate of growth in the United States economy was already great; in the election campaign of 1960, Senator Kennedy's main theme was that if elected he would "get this country moving." He spoke of a 5% growth rate as a reasonable target. Active efforts to step up the rate of growth are in direct conflict with the adjustment process required to remove a payments deficit, at least according to the traditional view.

In short, the United States was unwilling to apply the classical remedies. When the balance of payments deficits and the accompanying gold outflows caused bank reserves to fall, we did not allow a fall in the money supply to take place. Instead, the Federal Reserve System counteracted or offset the effect of the gold drain on bank reserves. It did this by open-market operations— that is, it bought government bonds in the open market, thus replenishing the reserves of commercial banks. This action can clearly be seen in the reported figures, as shown in Table 7-3. Far from reducing the money supply, the Federal Reserve System took action to expand bank reserves and thus permit an *expansion* of the money supply. As the gold stock fell $12.4 billion from 1957 to 1968, the Federal Reserve bought Treasury securities and expanded credits by $28.5 billion. United States policy was clearly aimed at domestic objectives, and the Federal Reserve allowed the money supply to rise as output expanded. In spite of the payments deficit the money supply rose $57 billion between 1957 and 1968—from $136 billion to $193 billion.

Table 7-3. Selected Monetary Variables, United States (Billions of Dollars)

	United States Securities held by Federal Reserve	Gold Stock	Member Bank Reserves	Supply of Money
December 1957	24.0	22.8	19.4	135.9
December 1962	30.5	16.0	20.0	147.5
December 1968	52.5	10.4	27.3	193.1

Source. *Federal Reserve Bulletin.*

Nor did we use fiscal policy to apply deflationary pressure. Government expenditures rose steadily from 1958 to 1968, exceeding tax revenues in every year. Even so, unemployment rates remained uncomfortably high during the first half of this period, and in 1963 taxes were sharply reduced in an effort to stimulate the economy. This action was called a "declaration of independence from balance of payments discipline," since it, like our monetary policy, ran counter to the traditional behavior expected of a deficit nation. Instead of deflating domestic demand, we were expanding it. In 1968 a tax surcharge was passed in an effort to reduce the growing inflationary pressures, but the gross national product rose from $445 billion in 1958, to $632 billion in 1964, and to $861 billion in 1968.

In one respect, we did follow the classical prescription. We allowed our short-term interest rates to rise in order to encourage foreigners to hold dollar balances. A rule was changed to permit banks to pay higher interest rates on time deposits. The original plans was to hold the long-term interest rate steady at about 4%, but to allow the short-term rate to rise. This plan, known as "operation twist," appeared to be working from 1960 to 1965, but thereafter the growth in aggregate demand led to inflationary pressures in the United States, and both long and short-term interest rates moved sharply higher after 1965. The transition year was 1965, as may be seen in Figure 7-4.

From 1958 to 1964, the United States enjoyed remarkable price stability, and wage increases largely stayed within the range of increases in productivity. During this period our principal competitors in Europe had larger increases in prices and wages than we did, and our competitive position therefore improved. This

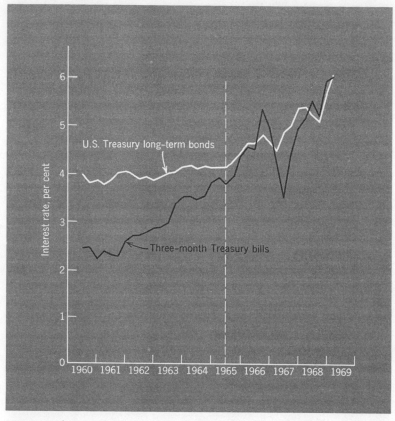

Figure 7-4. Behavior of short-term and long-term interest rates in the United States, 1960 to 1968. Until mid-1965, the long-term rate remained steady, while the short-term rate rose, in response to "operation twist." In 1965, the long-term rate also rose as inflationary pressures gathered force. *Source. Federal Reserve Bulletin.*

can be seen in the trade statistics: United States merchandise exports rose from $16 billion in 1958 to $25 billion in 1964, while imports rose only from $13 billion to $19 billion. The United States surplus on current account (transactions in goods and services) rose from $2.3 billion in 1958 to $8.5 billion in 1964.

This dramatic improvement in the United States current account balance also resulted, in part, from a number of expenditure-switching policies that were adopted after 1958. The tariff-free tourist allowance was cut from $500 to $100; this was done in the hope that United States tourists would spend less in foreign countries and perhaps even decide to vacation in the United States. A campaign was also launched to increase foreign tourism in the United States. All government expenditures abroad were carefully scrutinized, and domestic goods and services were purchased instead of foreign ones, unless the domestic price exceeded the foreign one by a large margin (50% for defense procurement). United States merchandise replaced foreign items in United States Army post exchanges; United States ships were used for all government cargo; foreign aid recipients were required to spend aid funds in the United States; and dependents of military personnel were asked to stay home when the head of a family was posted abroad. At the same time, United States business firms were urged to expand their foreign sales. The government sought to supply better information on foreign market opportunities and improved credit facilities for financing export sales. These various actions probably had some modest effect on our trade balance, but the major cause of the improvement was the rise in European prices and wages at a time when United States prices stayed constant. It is interesting that the adjustment in the current account took place largely in the *surplus* countries, not in the deficit country. Europeans were well aware of this, and they argued that they should not be expected to undergo inflation in order to correct our deficit.

Despite the enormous improvement in our current account between 1958 and 1964, the *over-all* balance-of-payments deficit remained at an uncomfortably high level. There are two principal reasons for this rather paradoxical situation.

First, the accounting definition of a "deficit" used by the Department of Commerce tends to put the United States position in the worst possible light. We discussed this point in Chapter 4, observing that the 1964 balance of payments showed a small surplus on one definition, but a $3 billion deficit on the Department of Commerce definition. However, since world attention is focused on the deficit as measured by Commerce, to restore confidence in the dollar we must eliminate the deficit on that definition.

Second, the more important reason for the continued deficit is that the outflow of capital from the United States to the rest of the world rose greatly over the period from 1958 to 1964. Government loans and grants (foreign economic aid) rose a little, but the big increase was in private foreign investment. United States firms increased their direct investment in foreign industry, building new plants or buying existing ones in Canada, the United Kingdom, Common Market countries, and many others. Such investments have been extremely profitable, and the return flow of interest and profits is an important credit item in our balance of payments, but when the investments are made they do increase the supply of dollars in the foreign-exchange market. The international bond market also revived in the 1958 to 1963 period, and a growing volume of foreign bonds was issued in the New York capital market. The efficient operation of the New York market combined with relatively low interest rates and readily available funds to cause a sharp rise in foreign borrowing in the United States.

Foreigners complained that the United States was "lending long and borrowing short," and thereby profiting at their expense. There was an element of truth in this charge, since the outflow of United States funds for direct investment, bond purchases, and bank loans contributed to the excess supply of dollars in the foreign exchange market. When foreign central banks acquired these dollars as a result of their support of exchange rates, they were in effect "lending" to the United States on a short-term basis.[6]

When the United States payments deficit continued at a high level despite the great improvement in our current account balance, the government finally took steps to check the outflow of capital. From 1963 to 1968 the United States acted, with increasing severity, to check the outflow of capital. The first dramatic

[6] When Chrysler buys into Simca, the French automobile firm, for $100 million, the Bank of France may acquire an additional $100 million which it holds in a time deposit earning 4% interest. The Bank of France is virtually forced to buy the dollars because of its responsibility to stabilize the franc-dollar exchange rate. The net effect of the transaction is that the United States acquires a share of French industry and France acquires a dollar deposit on which it earns a low rate of interest.

move was the imposition of a so-called "interest equalization tax" in 1963. United States residents who bought foreign bonds and stocks had to pay a tax of 15% of the purchase price.[7] This tax brought European bond issues in New York to a sudden halt, but the outflow of capital then began to take other forms, and additional restrictions (on bank loans and direct investments) were imposed, culminating in a drastic package of restrictions announced by President Johnson on January 1, 1968. This package, which utilizes mandatory controls along with "guidelines," represented a substantial increase in government control of foreign investment.

As we have seen, the outflow of capital rose from 1958 to 1964, and thus offset the United States surplus on current account. After 1964, however, prices and wages began to rise in the United States, imports increased at a faster rate than exports, and the current account surplus dwindled. Indeed, by 1968 the $8.5 billion surplus enjoyed in 1964 had fallen to only $2.0 billion. Nevertheless, in 1968 the United States had its first overall balance-of-payments *surplus* since 1957! The primary reason for this apparent paradox is that a large inflow of foreign-owned capital occurred. Europeans found the record high interest rates in the United States very attractive, and they were also uneasy about the stability of several European currencies. U. S. corporations sold over $2.0 billion of dollar-denominated bonds in the Euro-bond market in 1968, and foreign buyers bought corporate stock through the New York markets.

Welcome though it was, the improvement in the United States balance of payments in 1968 was thought by many to be temporary and something of a fluke. The inflow of foreign capital could cease (or even be reversed) as quickly as it started, while the weakened current account position of the United States would be more difficult to reverse, especially in view of the stubborn inflationary pressures we faced.

On the other hand, the emergence of a modest surplus in the

---

[7] The tax rate was 15% for stock and for bonds maturing in 15 or more years; rates were lower for bonds of shorter maturities. Securities of underdeveloped countries were not subject to the tax, and an exemption was also provided for Canada.

U.S. balance of payments ($1.6 billion on the "official settlements" basis; $160 million on the "liquidity" basis) meant that the exchange reserves of other nations decreased in 1968. Although these nations had long complained about excessive dollar holdings and had chided the United States for its payments deficits, they clearly did not relish the consequences of our surplus. The need for an additional source of reserves—other than gold and national currencies—was again dramatized.

III. PROPOSALS FOR REFORM OF THE INTERNATIONAL MONETARY SYSTEM

People sometimes worry about a shortage of reserves, but they need not worry about a shortage of proposals for monetary reform, since these exist in bewildering variety. Monetary reform has always appealed to the lunatic fringe, and every monetary crisis brings out a flock of new proposals whose authors claim them as panaceas for the world's economic ills—much as patent medicines are offered as cures for everything from cancer to sterility. Even among the serious, legitimate proposals for reform, the choice is very wide. We shall describe four main variants (Sections III A to III D).[8]

Fundamentally, the two problems that all reform plans must somehow solve are (1) how to provide for suitable increases in world monetary reserves, and (2) how to provide for correction of deficits and surpluses in national balances of payments. Solutions to both of these problems require a compromise between national autonomy and international control, and the *political* aspects may be more important than the economic in determining the final choice.

A. *Increase the Price of Gold*

If the United States were to double the price at which it buys and sells gold, the money value of the world's accumulated stock of monetary gold would also double, rising from $43 billion to $86 billion (end-of-1968 figures). Moreover, many private hold-

[8] For a compact, informative discussion of these and other proposals, see Fritz Machlup, *Plans for Reform of the International Monetary System*, Special Paper No. 3 (revised), International Finance Section, Princeton University, March 1964.

ers of gold might then take their profits and sell their hoards of gold to central banks, further increasing monetary gold reserves. Such an enormous increase in the money value of gold reserves would provide ample international reserves for many years to come.

The annual value of newly mined gold, currently about $1.4 billion, would also double, so that needed increases in reserves would be supplied by gold mining. In fact, a rise in price from $35 to $70 per ounce would so greatly stimulate the gold-mining industry that the value of newly mined gold would probably more than double. Mines that are unprofitable at $35 per ounce would be highly profitable at $70 per ounce.

Advocates of an increase in the price of gold argue that gold could then entirely replace national currencies in the official reserves of every nation, thus eliminating the friction and instability arising from the threat of a run on gold, a sudden conversion of currencies into gold. Exchange rates need not change at all; other countries could also change the relation of their currencies to gold, leaving official par values in terms of dollars unaffected.

This proposal would certainly meet the first problem—that is, it would provide ample increases in total world reserves. Indeed, some opponents argue that such a large initial increase would be decidedly inflationary, since it would remove the external restraint now limiting domestic economic expansion in many countries. If all of them tried to expand, world productive capacity would be strained and prices would tend to rise.

By itself, a higher gold price does not solve the second problem. It provides no *new* adjustment mechanism for the correction of deficits and surpluses in national balances of payments. Some advocates of this solution, notably the French economist Jacques Rueff, want to see a return to the classical gold standard. However, they do not explain how governments are to be persuaded to let their domestic economic policies be firmly linked to changes in their gold reserves. Political resistance to the discipline of gold has been strong for over 30 years, and it is unlikely to vanish just because the price of gold rises.

Doubts on this score weaken the case for a return to gold, but numerous other objections are also made.

First, the United States opposes an increase in the price of gold because it has publicly committed itself to maintain the present price, and therefore feels a moral obligation to those nations that have believed the United States pledges and kept reserves in dollars.

Second, the distribution of revaluation profits would be uneven, with the biggest gains accruing to nations that have weakened the present system by converting dollars into gold and the biggest losses accruing to the nations that have taken us at our word.

Third, Soviet Russia and South Africa would be the principal gold-producing beneficiaries of a higher price, and few people wish to confer large and recurring benefits on these two nations.

Finally, and most important to economists, there is no logical reason why the world should depend for its increments in monetary reserves upon the rate at which gold can be dug out of the bowels of the earth. Indeed, it seems purely wasteful to use productive resources—labor and capital—to dig up gold in one part of the world only to bury it in the vaults of central banks in some other (or the same) country. Incidentally, men have been protesting the foolishness of this behavior for at least 1500 years. Professor Viner finds St. Ambrose protesting in the fourth century, "You dig up gold from the veins of metal in the depths of the earth at the risk of life only to hide it away."[9] Modern economists repeatedly make the same comment about the absurdity of man's attitude and behavior toward gold, yet the hold of gold on the popular mind seems as strong as ever.

Most economists agree that a rational world would demonetize gold, removing it entirely from monetary reserves and letting it be bought and sold purely as a commodity, such as tin, copper, or platinum. Gold has already been eliminated from its former use in the domestic money supply of individual nations, but it still retains its function as a monetary reserve for use in settling international balances. (However, as we saw in Chapter 4, gold is not used in settling day-to-day transactions; it is limited to final, last-resort settlements between central banks.)

[9] Jacob Viner in *Gold, the Dollar, and the World Monetary System*, Committee for Economic Development, June, 1965, p. 12.

If gold were demonetized, most people think that its price would fall far below the present fixed price of $35 per ounce. Perhaps it would, but if governments would allow individual citizens to buy it freely, the price might soon recover. Indian peasants buy gold in the black market at twice the official price, and it is unlikely that their demand would be lessened by any action of central bankers in Atlantic nations.[10] Even in the United States, private demand might be considerable if individuals were allowed to hold gold.

Rational as it may be, demonetization of gold is unlikely to occur in the near future, if only because nations cannot agree on a system of managed reserves to replace it. Most reform proposals try to keep a place for gold in the system.

B. *Fluctuating Exchange Rates*

One proposal that does not retain a role for gold is the proposal that exchange rates be allowed to fluctuate freely in the market, and that governments cease all attempts to peg or stabilize the rates by direct intervention. Under this system the first problem is solved by eliminating it—that is, concern about an adequate level of international reserves would disappear because reserves would no longer be needed. Governments might still keep some working balances, but these would not be needed to finance deficits or to support a pegged exchange rate. The value of gold would depend upon its value as a commodity, as determined in the market.

Whether this system would provide a satisfactory mechanism of adjustment is a matter of debate.[11] Many economists believe that it would, and that changes in exchange rates would have powerful expenditure-switching effects, decreasing a deficit country's imports and increasing its exports. Others fear that, although

---

[10] There is a story about an eager graduate student conducting an opinion poll in a remote Indian village.

EAGER GRADUATE STUDENT: What do you think about American economic aid?

OLD INDIAN PEASANT: America? What is America?

EAGER GRADUATE STUDENT: Uh, do you think conditions are better since the British left?

OLD INDIAN PEASANT: The British? Who are the British?

[11] See also Chapter 4.

the accounting deficit would disappear, external disequilibrium would simply show up in another form—perhaps in chronic inflation and exchange-rate depreciation. They also argue that every action of government will have an influence on the exchange rate. Even if the government does not support the rate directly, its other actions will, increasingly, be calculated to keep the rate stable. Consequently, governments will not really have a freer hand to conduct domestic policy than they have under a fixed exchange rate system.

The great attraction of the fluctuating exchange rate system is its simplicity. With one stroke we could sweep away the vast apparatus of pegged exchange rates, stabilization funds, reserve-creating machinery, credit arrangements among central banks, worries about a run on gold, and arguments about the benefits and costs of key currencies. In a world in which domestic prices and incomes cannot be reduced to correct an external deficit, the attempt to maintain fixed exchange rates simply guarantees the continuation of the deficit. Allowing exchange rates to move freely would at least restore some flexibility to the system.

Opponents argue against freely fluctuating exchange rates on several grounds. First, they say that fluctuating exchange rates would be disturbing to ordinary trade and investment because they would add to uncertainty and risk. Second, large and frequent charges in exchange rates would cause wasteful resource movements because they would shift the margin of comparative advantage. Third, changes in an exchange rate would tend to cause further changes in the same direction. Depreciation of the pound, for example, would increase the price of imported goods in the United Kingdom and thus put upward pressure on internal prices and wages. If prices and wages are allowed to rise, the beneficial effect of exchange depreciation on the trade balance will be offset, and further depreciation will become necessary. Fourth, speculation may cause an exchange rate to rise or fall more than is warranted by the "true" economic situation, producing still more wasteful resource movements.

All of these points are vigorously denied by advocates of fluctuating exchange rates. The debate has been lengthy, heated, and inconclusive. Economists are divided on the issue, but a growing number of them now favor fluctuating rates. Practical men—businessmen, bankers, and government officials—have been almost solidly in favor of fixed rates, but one can now detect a more receptive attitude toward proposals to introduce a greater degree of exchange rate flexibility into the system. However, it is quite unlikely that fluctuating exchange rates will be deliberately adopted in the foreseeable future. Only if a severe financial crisis destroys the fixed-exchange rate system are we likely to see much use of fluctuating rates.

C. Centralization of International Monetary Reserves

Many reform proposals seek to modify the present system in order to improve its operation, while retaining most of its essential features. One class of proposals goes in the direction of a world central bank, which would perform functions for the world as a whole similar to the functions performed for the nation by its national central bank. Such a world bank would hold the reserves of each member nation, and it would have the power to create new reserves as needed by the world economy. The best-known proposal of this type is the one put forward by Professor Robert Triffin.[12] Triffin's scheme is similar in some respects to a proposal made in 1943 by John Maynard Keynes.[13] These plans are complex because they must provide for a wide range of contingencies and because the operating details must be spelled out with great care. However, the basic principles of their operation are extremely simple. We shall concentrate on the way in which the two basic problems are met: provision of adequate monetary reserves and a mechanism for correction of deficits and surpluses.

If a world central bank were created, or if the IMF were expanded to give it central banking powers, individual nations could hold their reserves in the form of deposits in the new international organization—for brevity, call it the XIMF, as Oscar Altman has done. Nations could transfer their existing reserves of dollars, pounds, and even gold to the XIMF, receiving in exchange a deposit credit on the books of that organization. This transfer would immediately eliminate the instability in the present

[12] See his *Gold and the Dollar Crisis* (New Haven: Yale University Press, 1960).
[13] Keynes' plan is reprinted in H. Grubel, *World Monetary Reform* (Stanford: Stanford University Press, 1963).

Table 7-4.

XIMF (Billions of Dollars)

Assets		Liabilities	
Gold	$20	Deposits of member	
Dollar balances	13	nations	$42
Sterling balances	6		
Other balances	3		
	$42		$42

system caused by the fact that nations now hold much of their reserves in national currencies in which they do not have full confidence. *If* nations have confidence in XIMF deposits and are willing to hold their reserves in that form (a very large "if"), one major weakness in the present system would be solved.

The big, practical question is how to inspire that confidence, how to set up the XIMF so that nations will have perfect trust in it. Triffin sought to win confidence by making the deposits at XIMF convertible into gold, but that would be difficult. Ultimately, the problem of confidence depends on binding commitments by member nations to keep their reserves in the XIMF, and to accept XIMF deposits as final payment from other countries for amounts due. Such permanently binding commitments run into conflict with national sovereignty—any treaty can be abrogated by the signatory governments—hence perfect confidence is difficult to achieve.

If nations ever could bring themselves to make the necessary commitment to an XIMF, its operating principles would be simple. If all reserves in national currencies and, for example, $20 billion of gold reserves were transferred to the XIMF, its balance sheet would appear as shown in Table 7-4.[14] The XIMF could then function as a closed-circuit banking system. That is, if Italy had a deficit vis-à-vis France, Italy could cover its deficit by transferring part of its XIMF deposit to the account of France. Total outstanding deposits of the XIMF would remain the same.

Other nations would probably object to having XIMF deposits stated in dollars, and some other unit of account may have to be

[14] These figures are hypothetical.

Table 7-5.

XIMF (Millions)	
Assets	*Liabilities*
French securities purchased in the open market +$300	Deposit of France +$300

devised. Keynes called his unit the "bancor" and defined it in terms of gold. So did Triffin. The true problem here is to protect member nations against loss through exchange-rate depreciation. It should be possible to devise an exchange-rate guarantee to put this fear to rest.

Reserves held in this form should be free from the instability presently caused by the threat of sudden flights from dollars into gold, or from one national currency into another. As long as all nations accepted XIMF deposits, they would be "as good as gold," if not better.

The XIMF could also be empowered to *increase* total reserves of member nations. It could do so through open-market operations, just as a national central bank can increase domestic bank reserves. If world reserves were judged to be insufficient, the XIMF could buy short-term securities in national money markets, paying for them with credits to the deposit accounts of those nations. For example, if the XIMF bought $300 million worth of French securities, France's deposit in XIMF would rise by $300 million. The transaction on the XIMF ledger would simply show an equal increase in assets and liabilities, as listed in Table 7-5. The increase in France's XIMF deposit represents a net increase in total reserves. If France were to run a deficit and draw on this deposit, the deposit would be transferred to another nation but it would remain in the system.[15]

Since the XIMF's initial holding of dollar and sterling assets

[15] In the Keynes' plan, total reserves increased when member nations drew overdrafts on the XIMF, or the "clearing union" as Keynes called it. The important difference lies not in the technique of reserve expansion, however, but in the fact that in Keynes' scheme the *initiative* for reserve expansion remained in the individual member nation, while in the Triffin scheme the managers of the XIMF have the initiative.

would be large, it would probably want to expand reserves by buying assets in member countries other than the United States and the United Kingdom. Some economists have suggested that it should buy securities in underdeveloped countries, thus providing these countries with increased reserves which they could use to buy needed imports from advanced countries. Alternatively, the XIMF could buy World Bank bonds. Reserve expansion would then be combined with economic assistance to underdeveloped countries.

Such an expanded IMF could certainly provide whatever amount of international reserves the world might need. No serious technical difficulties exist. The real problems are largely political in nature. Who is to control the XIMF? Who has the power to decide how large an increase in world reserves is desirable? Precisely how will the increase be brought about? Keynes wanted to put a group of technical experts in charge, hoping thereby to avoid the straight political issues of conflicting national interests. Triffin suggested that, as a safeguard against excessive reserve expansion, a limit might be placed on expansion of reserves by the XIMF—for instance, 3% per year. Within that limit, however, he thought discretionary power should be lodged with the governing body of the XIMF. We are still very far from an agreement on the political aspects of a world central bank.

Creation of a world central bank would not automatically solve the second major problem: correction of deficits and surpluses. With fixed exchange rates, nations would remain under pressure to correct external deficits by adopting suitable domestic policies. A deficit nation would draw down its reserve deposit at the XIMF. The decline in its reserves would impose the same constraints upon it that declining gold and exchange reserves now impose.

It is possible, however, to endow the XIMF with power to encourage or even force the correction of deficits and surpluses. The XIMF could have the power to provide additional reserve deposits to a deficit nation on condition that the deficit nation take certain definite steps to correct its deficit. Similarly, the XIMF could be given power to induce surplus countries to make part of the adjustment, and thus share the burden. (Keynes suggested that part of the surplus country's deposit be *canceled* if it took no steps to reduce its surplus. The threat of cancellation would certainly be a powerful stimulus to increased imports!)

Political issues are also paramount in the choice among the many possible schemes for conferring power upon the XIMF to enforce a mechanism to correct deficits and surpluses. Indeed, the potential conflict with national autonomy is greatest in this area.

These political issues, obviously, lie at the heart of the problem of international monetary reform. The technical economic issues and the operating procedures are now well understood; they are not the prime source of controversy. The really urgent problem is to find enough agreement about the political issues to permit the economic system to function as well as it should.

It may be that agreement cannot be reached on the political conditions necessary for creation of an international central bank such as we have described. The world may not be ready for a full-fledged international money, distinct from gold and national currencies. Professor Mundell points out that no such monetary unit has ever been created; he believes that successful creation of such a unit to displace the dollar as a key currency is about as likely in the near future as the adoption of Esperanto to replace English as the language of the sea.[16] However, as we shall see below (Sect. IV), SDRs are at least a beginning.

D. *Central Bank Cooperation and Assistance*

While these ambitious reform proposals have been discussed, a number of more modest proposals have been advanced, looking toward modification and extension of the existing system. These proposals, some of which have been adopted and put into operation, range from simple expansion of central bank cooperation to more formal arrangements such as the proposed "collective reserve unit" (CRU).

Through "swap agreements," two central banks can increase exchange reserves at the stroke of a pen. For example, the Federal Reserve Bank of New York can credit the *Deutsche Bundesbank* with $2 billion in return for a credit of 7.3 billion marks (the mark equivalent of $2 billion) to its account on the books of the

[16] Robert Mundell, Hearings, Subcommittee on International Exchange and Payments, Joint Economic Committee, July 27–29, 1965.

Deutsche Bundesbank. Both nations would then have larger foreign-exchange reserves. The Federal Reserve Bank of New York could draw on its mark balance as required to finance a United States payments deficit, and the German bank could use its dollar balance to support the mark if that became necessary. Such swap agreements have been used extensively in recent years by central banks of a few advanced countries. One multilateral swap agreement totaling $6 billion was arranged on a "stand-by" basis under the auspices of the International Monetary Fund ("stand-by" means that the funds are not actually paid over but are available on call).

One consequence of swap agreements is that a larger number of national currencies have come to be used as foreign-exchange reserves. As we saw in Chapter 4, the dollar and pound sterling have been virtually the only currencies held in official reserves, but the use of swap agreements has caused marks, guilders, lira, Swiss francs, and French francs to be held as well. Many proposals have been made to strengthen this trend toward the use of more reserve currencies. Some countries resent the special role of the dollar, apparently believing that the United States somehow profits from it, and it may therefore be politically desirable to move toward a multiple-currency reserve system.

As used thus far, swap agreements have been short-term, emergency arrangements. It has been proposed that they be extended and made a permanent part of the system. Through swap agreements, expansion of IMF quotas, greater flexibility in the use of IMF resources, and emergency credits extended by cooperating central banks, massive funds have been mustered for support of currencies under speculative attack. In 1963 to 1964, over $2 billion was made available to enable Italy to weather a balance-of-payments crisis, and in 1964 over $4 billion was assembled in a matter of hours to support the pound sterling. Not all these funds were actually used; their very existence may be enough to scare off the speculators. In any case, central bank cooperation has helped to keep the present system going. Many observers deplore its *ad hoc*, unsystematic character, however, and want to replace it by formal agreements.

One interesting proposal is that a selected group of nations (usually the so-called "Group of Ten")[17] formally agree to hold

17 The Group of Ten includes ten IMF members: Canada, the United States,

their exchange reserves in a fixed proportion of gold and national currencies.[18] For example, each country might agree to limit its gold holding to 60% of its total exchange reserve, keeping the other 40% in national currencies of the other participating nations. At the end of 1964, the combined reserves of the Group of Ten (plus Switzerland) were $45.6 billion, of which $34.1 billion was in gold. If these countries agreed to a 60% gold ratio, reserves in national currencies could increase by $11.4 billion, to $57 billion. Moreover, as newly mined gold flowed into monetary reserves, the national currency component could rise $4 for every $6 in new gold.

In one variant of this proposal, a "collective reserve unit" (CRU) would be defined to consist of *fixed* percentages of the several currencies of participating nations—50% dollars, 10% pounds, 12% marks, 8% French francs, and so on. Nations would agree to hold part of their reserves in CRU, perhaps in the same ratios as above—60% gold, 40% CRU.[19] Deficit nations would settle their balances in a combination of gold and CRU, and surplus nations would be obliged to accept CRU in partial payment. Advocates of this scheme believe that it would remove the threat of a flight from national currencies into gold—the threat that plagues the present system. Advocates also argue that the CRU system is fair and equitable because all countries share the risk of gain or loss from a change in the price of gold in proportion to their total reserves, and because all countries have a part in the reserve-currency role. The percentage of each national currency in the CRU would depend on the economic importance of the country, as measured, for instance, by its GNP.

Many technical problems arise in connection with the CRU scheme, but they could, no doubt, be solved if nations had a strong desire to adopt it. One reason for the strong interest in the CRU plan is that French officials have made favorable comments

---

Belgium, France, Germany, Italy, Japan, The Netherlands, Sweden, and the United Kingdom. Switzerland is also closely associated with this group.

[18] Many variants of this scheme have been put forward. The best known are those of S. Posthuma, "The International Monetary System," *Banca Nazionale del Lavoro Quarterly Review*, September, 1963, and E. M. Bernstein, "A Practical Proposal for International Monetary Reserves," Model, Roland & Company *Quarterly Review*, 1963.

[19] In Bernstein's plan, CRU would be established through the International Monetary Fund.

about it. The United States has been cool to the idea, perhaps because it might reduce the importance of the dollar in the international monetary system, and perhaps because its immediate effect could be a big drop in the United States gold stock. (The latter point depends upon the method used to initiate the CRU. If every nation were required to move at once to a 60:40 ratio, the United States would have to sell about $6.5 billion of gold to get other currencies, since our (end-of-1964) exchange reserve of $15.9 billion was almost entirely in gold.)

All of these schemes for central bank cooperation and adaptation of the present system are primarily concerned with our first problem—creation of an adequate supply of international reserves. None of the schemes provides any new mechanism for the correction of balance-of-payments deficits and surpluses. Positive corrective measures remain the responsibility of the individual nation. The chief constraint on the deficit nation is that imposed by its loss of reserves; unless it is making an effort to correct its situation, it cannot expect much help or sympathy from other members of the group. In this sense, a nation is limited in practice in its ability to pursue independent monetary and fiscal policies, even though it retains full autonomy in theory.

Experience with central bank cooperation and mutual assistance has led to a tradition of "multilateral surveillance." The entire economic and financial situation of a deficit nation may be subjected to searching review and criticism by a group of experts from other nations. While these discussions are voluntary and informal and the groups have no power to force any action, the deficit country knows that vigorous assistance will not be forthcoming unless it provides satisfactory evidence that it is taking suitable domestic action to improve its position. These discussions are also constructive in that they permit some pressure to be brought to bear on the surplus countries to share in the adjustment process.

IV. A MODEST STEP FORWARD: SPECIAL DRAWING RIGHTS

Years of discussion, debate, and controversy about international monetary reform culminated in 1967 with the adoption by the

Board of Governors of the IMF of the so-called Rio Agreement for a new facility—Special Drawing Rights.[20] The agreement is modest in scope, but it has far-reaching significance because it provides for the creation of a new kind of international money, and because nations have committed themselves to accept this new money.[21] Thus, the world need no longer depend solely upon gold and national currencies for its supply of international reserves.

To explain this new facility, we shall first need to explain briefly the regular quota and drawing right system. The original charter of the IMF provided that each member nation would be assigned a quota, the size of which was dependent upon the economic size of the country. The member nation is required to pay one fourth of its quota in gold or U.S. dollars, and the remaining three fourths in the national currency of the member nation. The IMF, therefore, has assets consisting of gold and dollars, plus a mixed bag of other national currencies. If a member nation has a deficit in its balance of payments, it can utilize its drawing rights under the IMF charter. That is, it can request a sum of money in a particular national currency. The funds drawn in this way can be used by the member nation to purchase the excess supply of its own currency being offered in the foreign-exchange market. For example, France can "draw" dollars from the IMF and use them to buy francs in the foreign-exchange market, thus covering its deficit. Technically, the member exercising its drawing rights pays in an amount of its *own* currency equivalent to the amount of the foreign currency drawn. When its balance of payments deficit is later corrected, the member nation is expected to reverse this transaction by using foreign exchange (that is, the currency of another nation) to repurchase the additional amounts of its own national currency that had been paid into the IMF. Thus, these drawing rights are similar to

[20] For a good discussion of the nature of this agreement and its implications for the future, see F. Machlup, *Remaking the International Monetary System—The Rio Agreement and Beyond* (Baltimore, 1968).

[21] Actually, the Rio agreement by the IMF Board of Governors must be ratified by the member governments. By the end of 1969, the necessary number of members had ratified, and the new facility began to operate Jan. 1, 1970.

short-term loans, and they are expected to be repaid. Furthermore, a member's right to exercise its drawing rights, beyond the first 25% of its quota, is dependent upon IMF approval. The first 25% of the member's quota, called the gold *tranche* (*tranche* is a French word meaning slice), is regarded in the original IMF agreement as part of the member nation's owned reserves, and the IMF cannot deny its use.

The existing quota and drawing right system has been briefly explained because the new plan for "special drawing rights" (SDR) builds upon these aspects of the existing machinery, but it also introduces significant differences. When the IMF decides to create a given amount of SDRs, say, $3 billion worth, the total amount created will be allocated among member nations in proportion to their quotas, as defined above. Once the distribution of SDRs has been made, a member has the right to draw against its allocation. These reserves are unconditionally owned by the member country; it need not obtain IMF approval in order to use these funds. However, it is expected that a member nation will not wish to draw against its SDRs except to cover a balance of payments deficit. The key feature of the new scheme is that other members are obliged to accept SDRs and to supply the equivalent amount of convertible currencies when asked to do so. These transactions may, in fact, be channeled through the IMF, and the IMF will probably decide which national currencies will be supplied to those nations exercising their drawing rights.

The reader can readily see that the method of allocating SDRs is a matter of vital interest to member nations. When a nation is given an allocation of SDRs, it acquires a claim on the rest of the world, and it can use its allocation to purchase real resources (goods, services, and assets). It was argued, for example, that newly created SDRs should be given to underdeveloped countries because of their great need for increased imports. When U countries used their SDRs to buy more goods and services, the new SDRs would in any case come into the hands of A countries. In the end, however, the A countries (who control the bulk of the voting power in the IMF) were unable to accept this plan, and the allocation was based on existing IMF quotas. In this method of allocation, the lion's share of a new batch of SDRs will

Table 7-6. Pro Rata Share of SDRs of Certain Member Nations (Millions of United States Dollars)

Nation	Existing IMF Quota	Share of $3.0 Billion of New SDRs
United States	$5,160	$729
United Kingdom	2,440	345
Germany	1,200	170
France	985	139
Canada	740	105
Japan	725	102
Australia	500	71
Burma	48	7
Chile	125	18
Ethiopia	19	3
India	750	106
Iraq	80	11
Mexico	270	38
Nigeria	100	14
Philippines	110	16
.	.	.
.	.	.
.	.	.
TOTAL	$21,224	$3,000

be received by A countries. Table 7-6 shows how much certain nations would receive from a $3.0 billion increment of SDRs.

Once an amount of SDRs has been created by the IMF, it will remain in existence and comprise a net addition to the world's supply of international reserves. When one nation uses its allocation of SDRs, another nation acquires that amount. This closed-circuit aspect of the special drawing rights clearly depends upon the willingness of member nations to accept SDRs. That willingness is signified by the ratification of this new agreement and by a decision to create additional SDRs. In view of the critical importance of this matter, the new agreement provides that an 85% majority of the total voting power in the IMF is required to create additional SDRs. This particular percentage was a source of much controversy in the negotiations leading up to this proposal, and the figure of 85% was adopted largely because the quotas of EEC members add up to somewhat more than 15%

and thus the EEC has a veto power over the creation of new SDRs. France was particularly insistent upon this point and called attention to the fact that the United States quota is so large that it has a veto power over actions for which an 80% majority is required.

As we have seen, the two-price system for gold means that the amount of gold held in the exchange reserves is frozen at the present level. We have also seen that nations are increasingly reluctant to add to their holdings of national currencies, especially the dollar. Now that the Rio agreement has been ratified and put into operation, we have, at last, a third kind of international reserves; one that can be created in whatever amounts may be desired or thought necessary by the member nations. Thus for the first time the world has a truly international money.

In late 1969 the·IMF announced that a decision has been made to create $9.5 billion of SDRs, $3.5 billion in 1970, and $3.0 billion each in 1971 and 1972. This decision was, of course, passed by the necessary 85% majority, and it means that SDRs will soon comprise a significant part of world international reserves. The price of gold in the free market responded by dropping sharply, to about $35 per ounce. Some observers predicted that it would fall even further, while others thought the price would hover around the $35 level. Whatever the outcome, it is clear that the world has taken a small step toward the demonetization of gold.

Index